sewing with nancy®

10•20•30 Minutes to
Sew *for your* Home

Nancy Zieman

Published by

Krause Publications
700 E. State St.
Iola, WI 54990-0001
Telephone 715-445-2214
www.krause.com

Please call or write for our free catalog of publications. Our toll-free number to place an order or obtain a free catalog is 800-258-0929 or please use our regular business telephone, 715-445-2214.

Nancy's Notions Editors: Pat Hahn, Amy Stalp
Project Designers: Donna Fenske, Kate Bashynski
Illustrator: Laure Noe
Photographers: Jim Gill, Dale Hall
Set Designer: Shirwil Lukes

Library of Congress Catalog Number: 2002105095

ISBN: 0-87349-530-6

Printed in the United States of America

Table of Contents

Selecting Fabrics

Selecting fabrics for a sewing project is always exciting! When you're choosing fabrics for one of these 10•20•30 Minutes to Sew for Your Home projects, you undoubtedly will want to begin by looking for firmly woven fabrics that complement other colors in your decorating scheme, as well as your decorating style.

• **Cotton Prints**—Many of the projects in this book feature cotton prints. Cotton prints are readily available in a wide range of colorations and designs, and they're both easy-sew and easy-care. Whether you're looking for a dainty floral print, a bold Southwestern motif, or a whimsical nursery design, you're sure to find something that fits your sewing needs.

If you select a lighter weight fabric, consider adding a layer of fusible interfacing to the wrong side of the fabric for added body and durability.

Instead of using a single fabric for each project, I've opted to combine several coordinates. For example, many of the projects showcase some of the 10 fabrics in my "Share the Love of Sewing" collection or the eight coordinates in my "Birds of a Feather" collection. You'll find lots of similar coordinates at your favorite sewing center.

Have fun experimenting with a variety of motif sizes. Use a combination of large, medium, and small prints, rather than restricting yourself to fabrics with designs of similar sizes.

But don't stop with cotton prints. The projects in this book also feature several specialty fabrics that are especially suited for sewing for your home:

• **Reinforced Plastic**—I like both the look and the sewability of this versatile fabric, featured on pockets of many of the projects. The see-through plastic base includes a fiberglass grid, which adds durability as well as a decorative touch. But more important, the fabric is much easier to sew than clear vinyl. If you've ever struggled trying to get vinyl to feed through your machine, give this fabric a try. I know you'll love it as much as I do. Cleanup is a breeze, too; just wipe it with a damp cloth.

• **Iron Quick Fabric**—This versatile fabric is made of 100% aluminum with a 100% cotton back. It's available both quilted and unquilted, with the quilted version layered with polyester batting backed with poly/cotton. Why do I like Iron Quick? The aluminized side reflects heat, making it ideal for projects like casserole carriers or pressing mats. The fabric is also easy care: machine wash cool/air dry flat, or use a damp cloth to clean the fabric.

• **Batting**—Usually hidden on the inside of a project, batting adds insulation to projects like casserole carriers, and it helps give loft and dimension to quilted projects. A polyester batting is appropriate for most projects, however I prefer a 100% cotton batting for projects like the Casserole Cozy. Cotton batting is not affected by the heat from a hot casserole dish, while a synthetic batting might be.

• **Oilcloth**—There was a day when oilcloth covered every kitchen table on the block. Now oilcloth is back with new technology and design. It's still water, stain, and soil resistant—just wipe with a warm soapy sponge. It's also lightweight, durable, and sturdy. Use it wherever you'd like a bold, stylish, washable surface. Have fun with this very versatile fabric!

• **High-loft fleece**—When you want cozy comfort and warmth without weight, 100% polyester high-loft fleece (fabrics such as Polarfleece® or Polartec®) definitely fit the bill. And because fleece doesn't ravel, edges don't need finishing. Several of the projects in this book use edge-joined seams, a technique that reduces bulk and makes the wrong side look as great as the right side. Caring for high-loft fleece couldn't be easier. Just machine wash warm and tumble dry low.

CHAPTER 1

Accessories for Your Sewing & Quilting Area

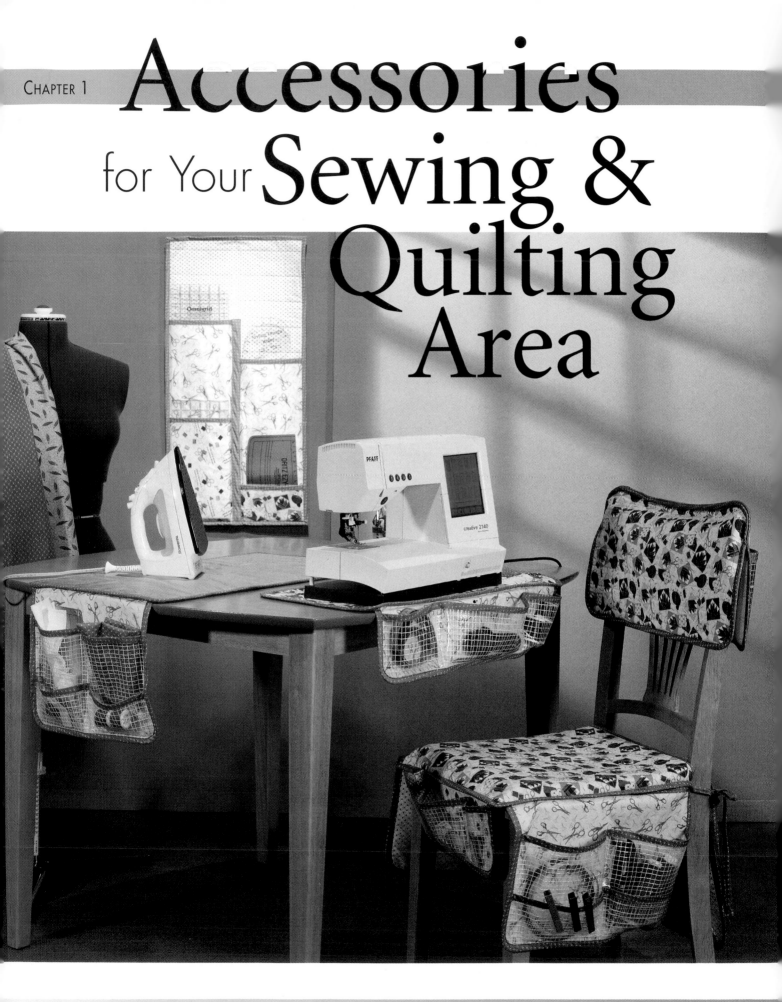

On the Go Machine Mat

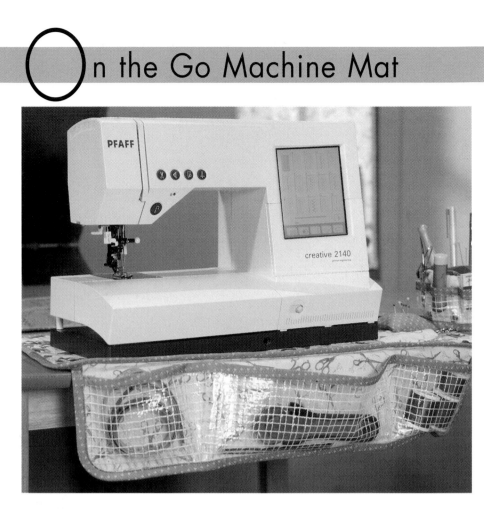

Transform a small space into an efficient sewing area with this functional sewing accessory. You can keep notions right at your fingertips in the easily accessible, see-through pockets. The mat cuts down on machine noise while protecting your tabletop and features a handy pincushion and a scissors pocket.

FINISHED MAT BASE

Approximately 12" x 24". Feel free to modify the size to accommodate the size of your machine and/or table.

MATERIALS NEEDED

- ¾ yd. Fabric A
- ¼ yd. Fabric B
- ⅜ yd. Fabric C
- ¼ yd. Reinforced Plastic
- ⅜ yd. batting
- ¼ yd. fusible interfacing

Making the Machine Mat

1. Cut out the fabric pieces using a rotary cutter, **20** ruler, and cutting mat.
   - Fabric A: Cut two 12" x 24" rectangles (mat base).
   - Fabric B: Cut two 6" x 22" rectangles (pocket panel).
     Cut one 3" x 6½" rectangle (scissors pocket).
   - Fabric C: Cut one 3½" x 6½" rectangle (pincushion).
     Cut nine or 10 bias strips 2" wide (binding).
   - Reinforced Plastic: Cut one 5" x 25" rectangle (pocket).
   - Batting: Cut one 12" x 24" rectangle (mat base).
   - Interfacing: Cut one 6" x 22" rectangle (pocket panel).

2. Prepare the mat base. **30**
   - Layer the two Fabric A rectangles and the batting; quilt the mat as detailed on page 90.
   - Round all four corners using a Radial Rule or a saucer.

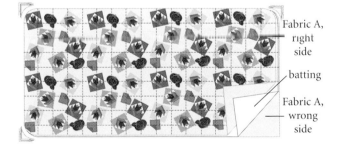

Fabric A, right side

batting

Fabric A, wrong side

3. Create a four yard length of bias tape from **15** Fabric C as detailed on page 92. Or purchase coordinating bias tape.

If you're planning to do more than one project from this chapter, save time by creating all the bias tape yardage you'll need at one time.

Nancy

4. Prepare the pocket.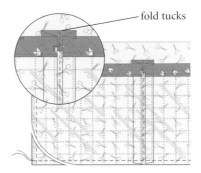
- Fuse interfacing to the wrong side of one Fabric B pocket.
- Meet the pocket panel sections, wrong sides together. Machine baste ¼" from the outer edges.
- Using a removable fabric marker, mark lines on the right side of the pocket panel 5½" from the left and right edges.

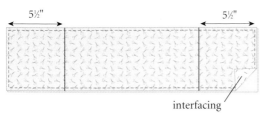

interfacing

- Bind the top edge of the Reinforced Plastic pocket as detailed on pages 92-96. Or use purchased coordinating bias tape.

bind top edge

- Mark lines 6½" from the left and right edges of the plastic pocket.

6½"   6½"

- Position the plastic pocket on the right side of the pocket panel, meeting the left, right, and lower edges. (The plastic section is wider than the background, so there will be excess plastic in the center. It will be pleated when the pocket is shaped.) Machine baste ¼" from the pocket left and right edges.

baste left and right edges

- Meet the marked lines on the Reinforced Plastic to those on the pocket panel. Machine stitch along the marked lines, dividing the section into three pockets.

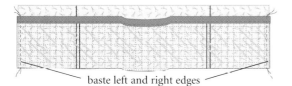

match markings; stitch

- Remove the excess fullness and add depth to the pockets by folding tucks on each side of the stitched lines, meeting the folds to the stitching lines.
- Machine baste ¼" from the lower edge. Round the two lower corners.

fold tucks

stitch; round corners

- Bind all except the top edge of the pocket panel as detailed on pages 92-96.

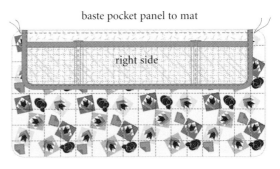

bind outer edges

5. Assemble the organizer. **30**
- Align the top of the pocket panel to one 22" edge of the mat, meeting the wrong sides and cut edges. Machine baste ¼" from the cut edges.

baste pocket panel to mat

right side

- Bind the outer edges of the mat as detailed on pages 92-96.

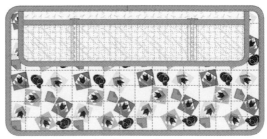

bind outer edge

6. Add a pincushion.
   - Meet the 3½" edges of Fabric C rectangle, right sides together. Stitch around the cut edges with a ¼" seam, leaving an opening for turning.

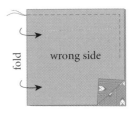

fold

wrong side

   - Turn the pincushion right side out, using a Bamboo Pointer and Creaser to gently push out the corners. Press.
   - Cut a 3" square of plastic such as Templar®. Insert the plastic inside the pincushion. The plastic prevents pins from going through the bottom of the pincushion and damaging the surface under the mat.

insert plastic

   - Stuff the pincushion with fiberfill, placing the fiberfill on top of the plastic base.

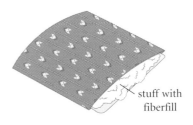

stuff with fiberfill

   - Hand stitch the opening closed.

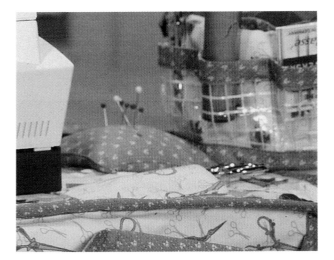

   - Position the pincushion on the right edge of the sewing mat, plastic side down, approximately 4½" from the bottom edge and 1½" from the right edge. Hand stitch in place.

7. Add a scissors pocket.
   - Meet the 3" ends of the Fabric B pocket rectangle, right sides together. Stitch around the cut edges with a ¼" seam, leaving an opening for turning.

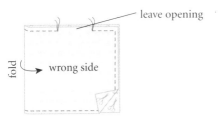

leave opening

fold

wrong side

   - Turn the pocket right side out, gently pushing out the corners with a Bamboo Pointer and Creaser. Press the pocket; hand stitch the opening closed.
   - Position the pocket on the sewing mat approximately 1½" from the bottom edge and 3" from the right edge. Machine stitch around three sides, leaving the right end open for inserting a scissors.

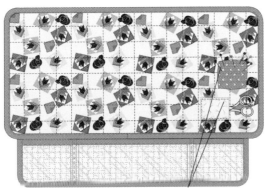

position pincushion and pocket

Create one of these mats for your sewing machine and a second one for your serger. Since many sergers have a narrower base, consider making the mat smaller.

Nancy

This pressing mat provides a usable pressing surface right next to your sewing machine—or anywhere else you want it, for that matter. Our mat includes four pockets, perfect for storing pressing tools such as Bias Tape Makers, a press cloth, Pocket Curve Template, and an Ezy-Hem® Gauge. Customize the number and size of pockets to fit your own pressing needs.

FINISHED PRESSING SURFACE:

15" x 26"

MATERIALS NEEDED

- ½ yd. Fabric A
- ⅜ yd. Fabric B
- ⅜ yd. Fabric C
- ¼ yd. Reinforced Plastic
- ½ yd. Iron Quick Fabric
- ½ yd. muslin
- ⅞ yd. 45" wide cotton batting
- ⅜ yd. fusible interfacing
- *Optional:* ¼ yd. Velcro®

Pressed for Time Pressing Mat

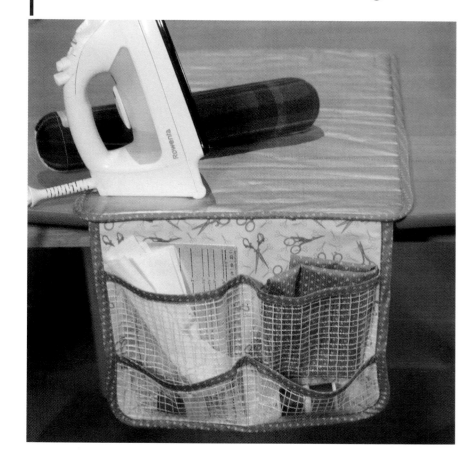

Making the Pressing Mat

1. Cut out the fabric pieces using a rotary cutter, cutting mat, and ruler. **20**
- Fabric A: Cut one 16" x 28" rectangle (mat backing).
  Cut one 11" x 13" rectangle (pocket lining).
- Fabric B: Cut one 11" x 13" rectangle (pocket base).
- Fabric C: Cut 10 or 11 bias strips 2" wide (binding).
- Reinforced Plastic: Cut one 4" x 15" rectangle (pocket).
  Cut one 8" x 15" (pocket).
- Iron Quick: Cut one 15" x 27" rectangle.
- Muslin: Cut one 16" x 28" rectangle.
- Cotton batting: Cut two 16" x 28" rectangles.
- Fusible interfacing: Cut one 11" x 13" rectangle.

2. Layer and quilt the muslin, two layers of batting, and the Fabric A mat backing as detailed on page 90. **30**

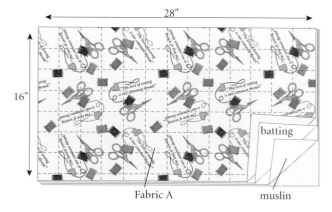

Fabric A   muslin

3. Prepare the mat base. **10**
- Place the quilted section right side down, with the muslin on top. Position the Iron Quick Fabric, aluminum side up.
- Pin the layers together; square up the mat to measure 15" x 27". Machine baste ¼" from the outer edges.

• Round all four corners using a Radial Rule or a saucer.

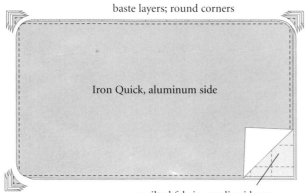

baste layers; round corners

Iron Quick, aluminum side

quilted fabric, muslin side up

4. Create a four yard length of bias tape from Fabric C as detailed on page 92. Or purchase coordinating bias tape.

15

5. Prepare the pockets.
• Fuse interfacing to the wrong side of the Fabric B pocket base. Stack and pin the pocket base and pocket lining, wrong sides together, meeting the outer edges. Machine baste ¼" from the outer edges.

30

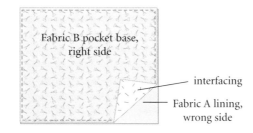

Fabric B pocket base, right side

interfacing

Fabric A lining, wrong side

• Bind the top edge of each Reinforced Plastic pocket as detailed on pages 92-96.

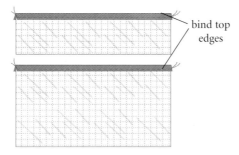

bind top edges

• Fold the fabric pocket panel in half, meeting the 11" edges. Press mark the center of the panel.
• Mark the center of each plastic pocket.

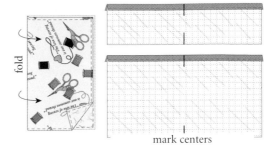

fold

mark centers

• Position the larger plastic pocket over the pocket base, meeting the marked centers and lower edges. Place the smaller plastic pocket over the larger pocket, meeting the center lines and lower edges. Machine stitch along the center marking, sewing from the binding edge to the cut edge.

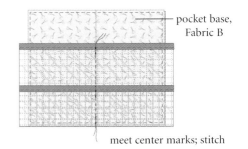

pocket base, Fabric B

meet center marks; stitch

• Meet the left and right edges of the Reinforced Plastic pockets to the pocket base. (The pocket sections are wider than the base, so there will be excess plastic in each pocket. It will be pleated when the pockets are shaped.) Machine baste ¼" from the left and right edges.

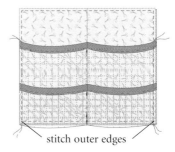

stitch outer edges

• Remove the excess fullness and add depth to the pockets by folding the tucks on each side of the stitched center line. Stagger the tucks in the large and small pockets to distribute the bulk.

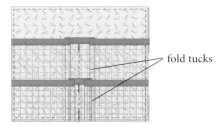

fold tucks

• Machine baste ¼" from the lower edge. Round the two lower corners using a Radial Rule or a saucer.

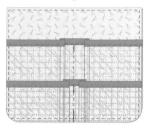

round corners

• Bind all except the top edge of the pocket panel as detailed on pages 92-96.

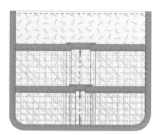

bind outer edges

6. Assemble the pressing mat. *20*
• Meet the wrong side of the pocket panel to one 15" edge of the Fabric A side of the mat, meeting the cut edges. Machine baste ¼" from the cut edges.
• Bind the outer edges of the mat as detailed on pages 92-96.

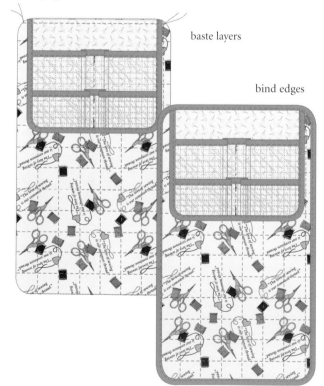

baste layers

bind edges

7. *Optional:* Add Velcro to attach the pressing *10* mat to the sewing machine mat (page 7).
• Cut a 9" length of Velcro.
• Position and stitch the loop side of the tape on the Iron Quick side of the pressing mat, placing it 2" from the lower left corner. Align the tape along the stitched edge of the binding.
• Position and stitch the hook side of the tape on the underside of the machine mat, placing it 2" from the lower right corner. Align the tape along the stitched edge of the binding.

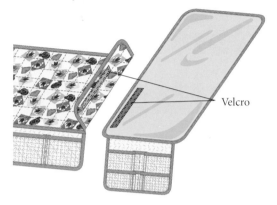

Velcro

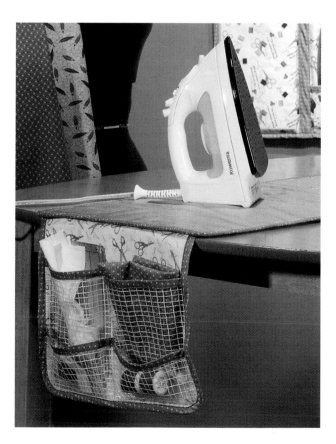

![M]ade to Order Ruler Organizer

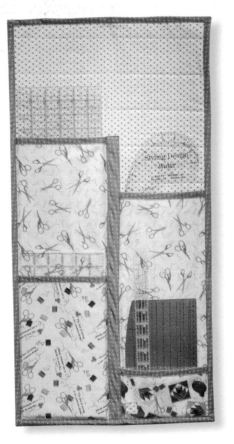

If you're at your wit's end trying to find a place for all your quilting rulers, this ruler organizer is just what you're looking for! Customize the size and number of pockets to accommodate your ruler supply. The organizer protects your rulers from scratches and breakage. Hang the organizer on the wall to save valuable table space, or fold it up and use the convenient handles to carry it to class.

FINISHED SIZE

Approximately 15" x 30"

MATERIALS NEEDED

- ½ yd. Fabric A
- ¼ yd. Fabric B
- ¼ yd. Fabric C
- ⅝ yd. Fabric D
- ⅜ yd. Fabric E
- ½ yd. Fabric F
- ½ yd. batting
- 1 yd. fusible interfacing

Making the Ruler Organizer

1. Cut out the fabrics. **20**
- Fabric A: Cut one 16" x 31" rectangle (organizer lining).
  Cut one 6" x 13" rectangle (rod pocket).
- Fabric B: Cut one 7½" x 8" rectangle (pocket).
- Fabric C: Cut one 7½" x 22" rectangle (pocket).
- Fabric D: Cut one 7½" x 42" rectangle (pocket).
  Cut one 7½" x 34" rectangle (pocket).
  Cut two 3" x 27" rectangles (carrying straps).
- Fabric E: Cut 10 bias strips 2" wide (binding).
- Fabric F: Cut one 16" x 31" rectangle (base).
- Batting: Cut one 16" x 31" rectangle (base).
- Fusible interfacing: Cut two 3" x 27" rectangles (carrying straps).
  Cut one 7½" x 21" rectangle (pocket).
  Cut one 7½" x 17" rectangle (pocket).
  Cut one 7½" x 11" rectangle (pocket).
  Cut one 7½" x 4" rectangle (pocket).

2. Layer and quilt the organizer base, using Fabric A, batting, and Fabric F, as detailed on page 90. Square the quilted base to 15" x 30". **30**

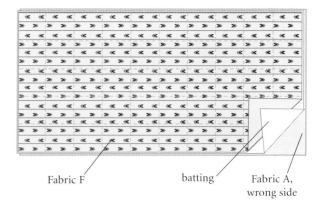

Fabric F   batting   Fabric A, wrong side

3. Prepare 4½ yards of binding from Fabric E as detailed on page 92. Or purchase coordinating bias tape. **15**

4. Add pockets to the organizer.
30
- Fold each pocket in half, wrong sides together, meeting the 7½" ends. Press the fold.
- Fuse interfacing to the wrong side of each pocket, aligning the edge with the pressed fold.
- Refold the pockets; bind the folded edges as detailed on pages 92-96.

wrong side — interfacing

- Arrange the ruler pockets on the base.
  - Mark a center line on the Fabric F base, extending the line as far as the longest pocket.
  - Layer the pockets in the desired configuration, placing the shorter pockets on top of the longer pockets. Align the pockets ⅛" from the center line and the outer edges of the organizer. (This provides space for the thickness of the ruler.) Machine baste in place, removing the excess fullness with tiny tucks along the bottom edge.

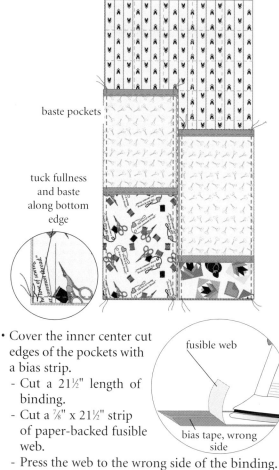

baste pockets

tuck fullness and baste along bottom edge

- Cover the inner center cut edges of the pockets with a bias strip.
  - Cut a 21½" length of binding.
  - Cut a ⅞" x 21½" strip of paper-backed fusible web.
  - Press the web to the wrong side of the binding.
  - Fold under and press ½" on one short end of the binding. Align the pressed end even with the top edge of the pocket binding, centering the binding over the guideline between the pockets. Press to fuse in place.

fusible web

bias tape, wrong side

- Edgestitch along the outer edges of the binding.

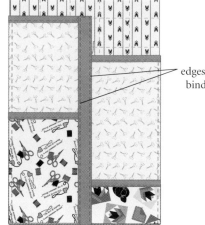

edgestitch binding

5. Prepare and attach the carrying straps.
10
- Fuse interfacing to the wrong sides of the straps.
- Meet the lengthwise edges of the straps, right sides together. Stitch a ¼" seam along the lengthwise edge.

stitch lengthwise edge

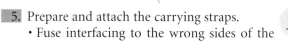

- Turn the straps right side out. Press the tubes flat, centering the seams.

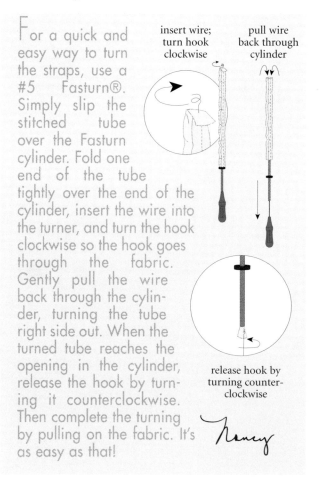

For a quick and easy way to turn the straps, use a #5 Fasturn®. Simply slip the stitched tube over the Fasturn cylinder. Fold one end of the tube tightly over the end of the cylinder, insert the wire into the turner, and turn the hook clockwise so the hook goes through the fabric. Gently pull the wire back through the cylinder, turning the tube right side out. When the turned tube reaches the opening in the cylinder, release the hook by turning it counterclockwise. Then complete the turning by pulling on the fabric. It's as easy as that!

insert wire; turn hook clockwise

pull wire back through cylinder

release hook by turning counter-clockwise

Nancy

- Add two to four rows of topstitching to each strap to add strength and stability.

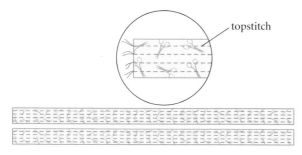

topstitch

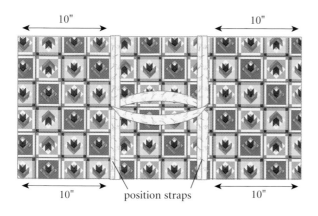

- Position the straps on the opposite edges of the Fabric A side of the organizer 10" from the short ends, meeting the cut edges. Baste in place.

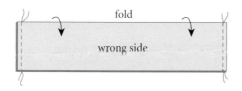

10"   10"

10"   position straps   10"

6. Add a rod pocket.
   - Fold the rod pocket in half, right sides **10** together, meeting the long edges. Stitch across the short ends with a ¼" seam.

fold

wrong side

- Turn the pocket right side out; press the seams and the center fold.

- Center the rod pocket along the upper edge of the Fabric A side of the organizer, aligning the cut edges. Baste in place.

baste rod pocket

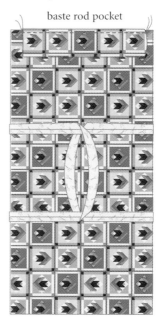

7. Bind the edges of the organizer, mitering the **30** corners as detailed on pages 92-96.

8. Hand stitch the folded edge of the rod pocket **5** 2½" from the bound edge.

hand stitch rod pocket

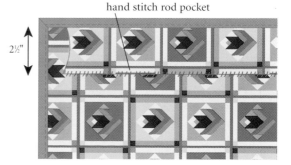

2½"

Ready, sit, sew! The cushioned seat of this Sit 'n Sew Chair Caddy lets you sew in comfort and style. Secure the caddy to a chair with convenient ties. The sides and front flap feature pockets galore that you can customize according to your needs. Your most-used tools will never be more than an arm's reach away.

On the back flap of the caddy, we added a larger pocket for storing books or patterns. This flap has a secret—there's a hidden pocket with an elasticized top edge and flap so you can safely store keys or a wallet without worry during a class.

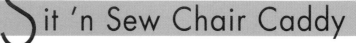

Sit 'n Sew Chair Caddy

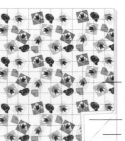

MATERIALS NEEDED

- 1 yd. Fabric A
- ½ yd. Fabric B
- 1 yd. Fabric C
- ½ yd. Fabric D
- ¾ yd. Fabric E
- ¾ yd. Reinforced Plastic
- ½ yd. batting
- ½ yd. elastic, ½" wide
- ⅞" x 20" strip of paper-backed fusible web
- ½ yd. 1" thick upholstery foam

Constructing the Chair Caddy

1. Cut out the fabrics.
   - Fabric A: Cut four 17" x 18" rectangles (pillow envelope).
   - Fabric B: Cut two 16" x 17" rectangles (pillow cover).
     Cut one 6" x 13" rectangle (front pocket lining).
   - Fabric C: Cut two 14" x 15" rectangles (back pocket base and lining).
     Cut four 11" x 16" rectangles (left and right pocket bases and pocket linings).
     Cut one 4" x 13" rectangle (hidden pocket flap).
   - Fabric D: Cut one 16" x 18" rectangle (hidden pocket).
     Cut one 6" x 13" rectangle (front pocket base).
     Cut one 4" x 13" rectangle (hidden pocket flap lining).
   - Fabric E: Cut 15 or 20 bias strips 2" wide (binding).
   - Reinforced Plastic: Cut two 8" x 18" rectangles (side pockets).

   Cut two 4" x 18" rectangles (side pockets).
   Cut one 13" x 16" rectangle (back pocket).
   Cut one 5" x 16" rectangle (front pocket).
   - Batting: Cut one 17" x 18" rectangle (pillow envelope).
   - 1" upholstery foam: Cut one 14" x 15" rectangle (pillow).

2. Prepare the panels for the pillow envelope.
   - Front panel: Layer the batting between the wrong sides of two 17" x 18" Fabric A rectangles. Quilt the panel as detailed on page 90. Square up the top to measure 16" x 17".

   layer and quilt front envelope panel

   Fabric A, right side

   batting

   Fabric A, wrong side

- Back panel: Meet and pin the remaining two 17" x 18" Fabric A rectangles, wrong sides together. Square to 16" x 17". Machine baste ¼" from the outer edges.

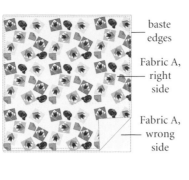

baste edges

Fabric A, right side

Fabric A, wrong side

3. Prepare approximately 14 yards of bias binding from Fabric E as detailed on page 92. Or purchase coordinating bias tape. **20**

4. Assemble the pillow envelope. **30**
   - Cut two 16½" lengths of binding for covering the opening edges of the envelope front and back. Bind one 16" edge of each section as detailed on pages 92-96. Edgestitch.

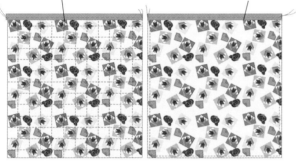

envelope front   bind upper edges   envelope back

- Bind the remaining edges of the envelope.
  - Align the bound edges of the upper and lower envelope sections. Machine baste ¼" from the unbound edges.

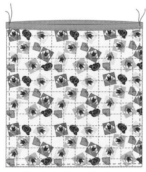

baste unbound edges

  - Mark the binding 18" from one end. This extension will become a tie.
  - Bind the three unbound edges as detailed on pages 92-96, using the two-step method.

18" extension
stitch binding to envelope back

Meet the mark on the binding to the aligned bound edges at the corner of the pillow envelope back. Miter the corners as you come to them.

- At the final bound edge of the envelope, mark the binding 18" beyond the corner. Cut the binding at that point to form the second tie.

edgestitch binding in place

  - Fold the binding to the upper pillow envelope and edgestitch the binding in place, beginning and ending at the ends of the ties.

miter corners

5. Add a hidden pocket to the back pocket lining. **30**
   - Meet the 16" edges of the 16" x 18" Fabric D hidden pocket, wrong sides together. Press the fold.
   - Stitch ⅝" from the fold to create a casing.

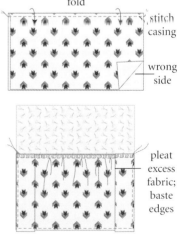

fold

stitch casing

wrong side

   - Insert a 13" piece of ½" wide elastic. Stitch across both the casing ends to secure the elastic.
   - Position the hidden pocket on the right side of the Fabric C back pocket lining, meeting the cut edges. Form pleats at the left and right pocket edges to remove the excess fullness. Machine baste ¼" from the cut edges.

pleat excess fabric; baste edges

   - Create a pocket flap.
     - Layer the 4" x 13" Fabric C pocket flap and the Fabric D pocket flap lining sections, wrong sides together. Machine baste ¼" from the cut edges. Round the corners using a Radial Rule or a saucer.

- Bind the curved edges as detailed on pages 92-96.
- Position the pocket flap over the hidden pocket; machine baste ¼" from the unbound edge.

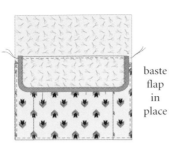

baste flap in place

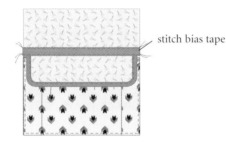

bias tape, wrong side

- Cut a 16" length of bias tape; cut a ⅞" x 16" strip of paper-backed fusible web. Press the web to the wrong side of the bias tape.
- Remove the paper backing and position the bias strip over the upper edge of the pocket flap. Press to fuse in place.
- Edgestitch along the edges of the bias tape.

stitch bias tape

6. Complete the back pocket panel. **30**
- Place the back pocket base over the back pocket lining, wrong sides together. Machine baste ¼" from the edges to secure the layers.
- Add a Reinforced Plastic pocket to the back pocket base.
  - Bind the top 16" edge of the 13" x 16" plastic pocket as detailed on pages 92-96.
  - Place the plastic pocket over the right side of the Fabric C back pocket base, meeting the cut edges. Machine baste ¼" from the left and right edges.

baste left and right edges

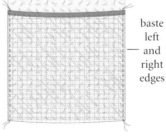

  - Remove the excess fullness by forming pleats at the left and right pocket edges. Machine baste ¼" from the lower edge. Round the corners using a Radial Rule or a saucer.

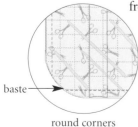

baste

round corners

- Bind the outer edge of the pocket, mitering the upper corners as detailed on pages 92-96.

7. Prepare the left, right, and front pocket panels using the same technique. **30**
- Add 8" and 4" Reinforced Plastic pockets on the Fabric C left and right pocket bases as detailed for the pressing mat on page 11, step 5.
- Bind the pocket panels, allowing an 18" extension at the left edge of the left panel and the right edge of the right panel.

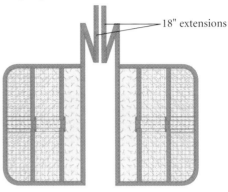

18" extensions

side pockets

- Add a 5" plastic pocket to the Fabric D front pocket base. Divide the Reinforced Plastic into three pockets, placing the pocket divisions 3½" from the left and right edges. Shape the pockets and round the lower corners as detailed above. Bind the pocket panel.

front pocket

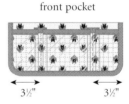

3½"   3½"

8. Attach the panels to the pillow envelope. **20**
- Place the pillow envelope, quilted side up, with the opening facing away from you.
- Pin the pocket panels to the underside of the pillow envelope, aligning the inner edges of the bindings.
  - Place the left and right pocket panels, pockets facing up, on the left and right sides of the envelope, with the back edges even. Position the panels so the ties are even with the pillow envelope ties.
  - Position the back pocket panel over the inside of the pillow envelope back panel.
  - Center the front panel under the front edge of the pillow envelope.

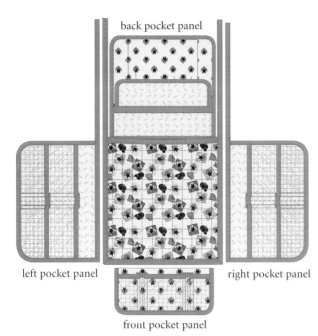

back pocket panel

left pocket panel

right pocket panel

front pocket panel

Here's an ideal place to use some of those utility stitches on your sewing machine. For example, try a triple straight stitch. The machine stitches three stitches forward, two back, then repeats that sequence. It's a great way to reinforce stitching and add durability.

Nancy

- Knot the ends of the ties.

9. Make a pillow to insert in the pillow envelope. **30**
   - Join the Fabric B pillow rectangles with a ½" seam, right sides together, leaving an opening for turning in the center of one side.
   - Miter each corner.

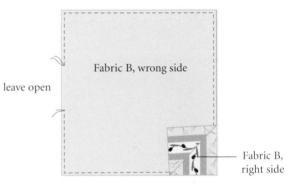

Fabric B, wrong side

leave open

Fabric B, right side

- Fold the corner so a triangular point forms, meeting the side seam to the top or bottom seam.
- Stitch across the lower edge of the triangle about 1" from the tip of the triangle. Reinforce the stitching at the ends.

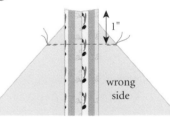

1"

wrong side

- Trim and finish the seam if desired.
- Turn the pillow cover right side out. Insert the upholstery foam, and hand stitch the opening closed.
- Slip the pillow into the pillow envelope for additional comfort.

- Secure the pocket panels to the pillow envelope with straight stitching, locking the stitches at the beginning and end of each line of stitching.
- Leave about 7" of each side pocket area unstitched as shown. This allows space for positioning the caddy around the sides of the chair.

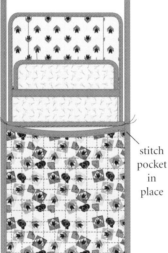

stitch pocket in place

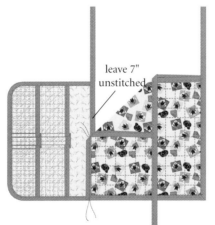

leave 7" unstitched

Add even more storage potential to your sewing area with this Chair Back Caddy. The padded cover slips easily over the back of a chair and lends an attractive accent …but that's not all. Four convenient pockets provide readily accessible storage for sewing notions or supplies.

FINISHED SIZE

Approximately 11" x 20"

MATERIALS NEEDED

- ⅜ yd. Fabric A
- ⅜ yd. Fabric B
- ⅜ yd. Fabric C
- ¼ yd. Reinforced Plastic
- ⅜ yd. batting

Chair Back Caddy

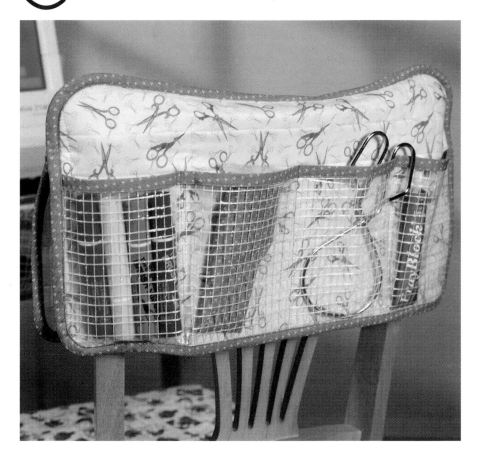

Making the Chair Back Caddy

1. Cut out the fabrics. **15**
   - Fabric A: Cut two 12" x 21" rectangles (front panel).
   - Fabric B: Cut two 12" x 21" rectangles (back panel).
   - Fabric C: Cut 10 or 11 bias strips 2" wide (binding).
   - Reinforced Plastic: Cut one 7" x 22" rectangle (pocket).
   - Batting: Cut two 12" x 21" rectangles (front and back panels).

2. Layer and quilt the front and back panels for the caddy as detailed on page 90. **20**
   - For the front panel, layer the batting between the two Fabric A rectangles.
   - For the back panel, layer the batting between the two Fabric B rectangles.

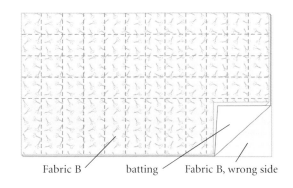

Fabric B   batting   Fabric B, wrong side

3. Prepare 4½ yards of binding from Fabric C as detailed on page 92. Or purchase coordinating bias tape. **10**

4. Add a pocket to the back panel.
 - Bind the top edge of the plastic pocket as detailed on pages 92-96.

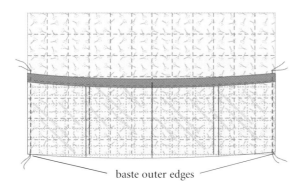

bind pocket edge

 - Divide the back panel into four equal vertical sections using an erasable fabric marking pen.
 - Divide the Reinforced Plastic pocket into four equal sections.
 - Position the plastic pocket over the back panel, meeting the left, right, and lower edges. (The pocket section is wider than the background, so there will be excess plastic in the pocket. It will be pleated when the pocket is shaped.) Machine baste ¼" from the left and right edges.

baste outer edges

 - Meet the pocket division marks to the panel division marks. Straight stitch from the binding edge to the cut edge along each marked line.

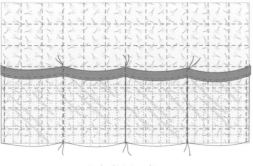

stitch division lines

 - Remove the excess fullness from each pocket by forming tucks along the stitched lines. Machine baste ¼" from the lower edge.

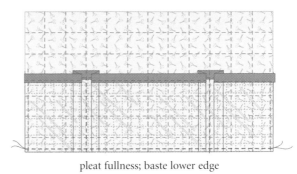

pleat fullness; baste lower edge

5. Round all four corners of each panel using a Radial Rule or a saucer. *5*

6. Bind the outer edges of the front and back panels as detailed on pages 92-96. *20*

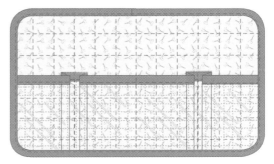

round corners; bind edges

7. Join the front and back panels. *5*
 - Meet the upper corners of the front and back panels, wrong sides together. Pin.
 - Stitch the two panels together using a utility triple straight stitch, following the edgestitching in the binding as a guide. Begin and end the stitching 3" from the upper corners.

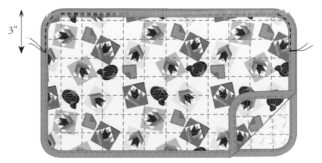

3"

stitch panels together

Design the Chair Back Caddy to fit the contour of your chair. Trace the shape of your chair back onto paper and use that as a pattern. Adjust the pockets accordingly for a custom fit.

Nancy

Mug Pinafore

Pour yourself a cup of notions, sit back, relax, and get ready to sew. Our Mug Pinafore can be sized to fit any coffee mug. It folds over the edge of the mug, creating two rings of pockets, both inside and outside. Use the attached ties to secure the pinafore to the mug for a snug fit. The pinafore is perfect for holding marking pens, a Little Wooden Iron, rotary cutters, seam rippers, and more! Make one for yourself, then make more as quick gifts for friends.

MATERIALS NEEDED

- ¼ yd. Fabric A
- ¼ yd. Fabric B
- ¼ yd. Fabric C
- ⅛ yd. Reinforced Plastic
- ⅛ yd. fusible interfacing

Note: *The above yardages and following instructions are appropriate for a mug approximately 3" high with a diameter of approximately 4½". Although yardages are listed above, this project is an ideal way to use fabric remnants from larger projects.*

Making the Mug Pinafore

1. Make a pattern for the pinafore.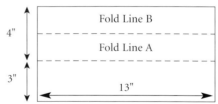
   - Measure the circumference of the mug, excluding the handle. Measure the height of the mug. Draw a rectangle on Pattern Paper that size. Label the upper long side "Fold Line A."
   - Double the mug height; subtract 2". Add this dimension above the long Fold Line A.
   - Divide the extension in half and draw a dotted line parallel to Fold Line A. Label this line "Fold Line B."

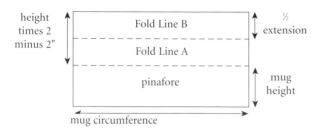

Example: If the mug measures 3" high and 13" around, the pattern will measure 7" x 13" and look like this:

	Fold Line B	
4"	- - - - - - - - - -	
	Fold Line A	
3"		
	13"	

- To make a pattern for the plastic pocket, subtract ½" from the mug height and add 5" to the mug circumference. The pocket pattern for the mug described above would measure 2½" x 18".

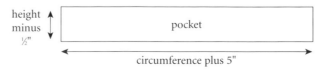

2. Cut out the fabrics for the mug pinafore (to fit a mug with the sample dimensions).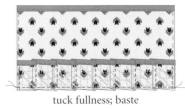
- Fabric A: Cut one 7" x 13" rectangle (pinafore front).
- Fabric B: Cut eight or nine bias strips 2" wide (binding).
- Fabric C: Cut one 7" x 13" rectangle (pinafore back).
- Reinforced Plastic: Cut one 2½" x 18" rectangle (pocket).
- Fusible interfacing: Cut one 3" x 13" rectangle.

3. Prepare approximately 2½ yards of bias binding from Fabric B as detailed on page 92. Or purchase coordinating bias tape.

4. Join the two sections of the pinafore.
- Fuse interfacing to the wrong side of the lower section of the Fabric A pinafore front.
- Layer the two pinafore sections, wrong sides together. Machine baste ¼" from the outer edges.

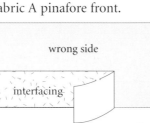

wrong side

interfacing

5. Bind the top edges of the pinafore and the plastic pocket as detailed on pages 92-96.

bind top edge

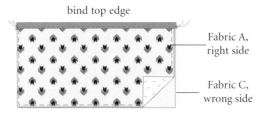

Fabric A, right side

Fabric C, wrong side

6. Add the Reinforced Plastic pocket to the pinafore.
- Divide the pinafore into eight equal sections using a removable fabric marking pen.
- Divide the plastic pocket into eight equal sections.

mark pocket sections

- Position the pocket over the pinafore front, aligning the left, right, and lower edges. Machine baste in place ¼" from the left and right edges.
- Align and machine stitch along each set of division marks, sewing from the bound edges to the cut edges. (The pocket sections are

baste outer edges

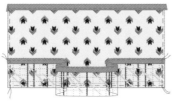

stitch pocket divisions

wider than the base, so there will be excess plastic in each pocket. It will be pleated when the pockets are shaped.)
- Remove the excess fullness by folding tucks in each mini-pocket; machine baste ¼" from the lower edge.

tuck fullness; baste

- Round the two lower corners using a Radial Rule or a saucer.

7. Add ties to the pinafore.
- Cut a 24" strip of bias binding. Fold the strip in half, meeting the folded edges. Press to create double-fold strips. Edgestitch.

fold

meet folded edges; edgestitch

- Cut the strip in half to form ties. Position the ties at the sides of the pinafore, about 1" from the lower edge. Baste in place.

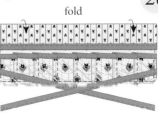

position and baste ties

8. Complete and bind the pinafore.
- Fold the bound edge of the pinafore toward the pocket side of the pinafore along Fold Line B. Machine baste ¼" from the left and right edges.

fold

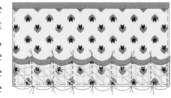

- Stitch the pocket divisions following the marked lines.
- Press under ½" at the end of the bias binding. Bind the outer edge of the pinafore as detailed on pages 92-96. When approaching the end of the pinafore, cut the binding ½" longer than the pinafore. Fold under the ½" extension and stitch the remainder of the binding in place.
- Knot the ends of the ties.

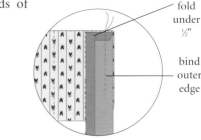

fold under ½"

bind outer edge

CHAPTER 2

Accessories
for Your Kitchen

Fold 'n Go Basket

Serve your next dinner in style by presenting fruits, breads, chips, or other taste-tempting foods in these unique baskets. Fold up the sides, fasten the buttons, and you're ready to go.

The baskets feature Reinforced Plastic for easy cleanup with just a wet cloth and a wave of your hand. With sides unbuttoned, you can store the flat baskets neatly in minimal space.

You can make this basket in less than two hours of sewing time, but when sewing time is limited, take an even easier approach. Divide the project into 10, 20, or 30 minute time periods, and voila! Your basket will be finished before you know it.

The following instructions make a basket approximately 8" square. You'll also find modifications for making a rectangular bread basket on page 29. Feel free to adapt these dimensions to suit your menu and your table.

Materials Needed

- ½ yd. Fabric A
- ⅓ yd. Fabric B
- ½ yd. Fabric C
- ½ yd. Reinforced Plastic
- ½ yd. batting
- Four ¾" to ⅞" buttons

Note: *You can make two baskets with these yardages. If you choose to make a second basket, you'll need a total of eight buttons.*

Making the Basket

1. Cut out the fabrics (for one basket). **20**
- Fabric A: Cut one 17" square (basket exterior).
- Fabric B: Cut 2" wide bias strips to total approximately 2 yards (binding).
  Cut one ⅞" wide 16" long bias strip (button loops).
- Fabric C: Cut one 17" square (basket interior).
- Reinforced Plastic: Cut one 17" square (basket lining).
- Batting: Cut one 17" square.

2. Layer and quilt the basket base using the 17" **20** squares of Fabric A, batting, and Fabric C as detailed on page 90. If the fabric has a natural grid as Fabric A does, follow that grid in quilting. Quilt as many or as few rows as you like.

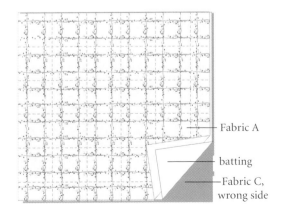

Fabric A

batting

Fabric C, wrong side

3. Shape the basket.

- Position the Reinforced Plastic over the Fabric C basket interior. Baste 2" at the center of each outer edge, stitching ¼" from the edge.

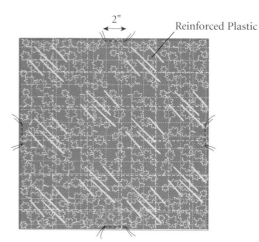

2"

Reinforced Plastic

- Square up the quilt sandwich. Trim away a 4" square from each corner.

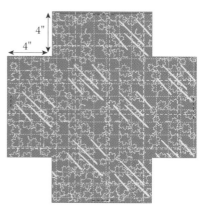

4"

4"

- Staystitch the inner corners a scant ½" from the cut edges. Clip into the interior corners without cutting through the staystitching.

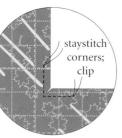

staystitch corners; clip

This staystitching has several functions. It keeps the layers together so it's easier to position and stitch the binding. It also reinforces the corner and provides a stitching guide for applying the binding. Clip close to, but not through, the corner. The closer you clip, the easier it will be to pivot and bind the inside corner.

Nancy

- *Optional:* Mark and stitch around the inner square from corner to corner to provide a folding line.

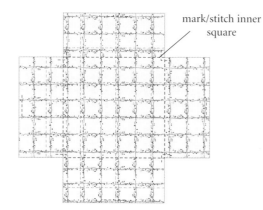

mark/stitch inner square

4. Prepare the button loops.
- Fold the ⅞" wide Fabric B bias strip in half, right sides together, meeting the long edges. Stitch a ¼" seam along the lengthwise edge, reducing the stitch length to 2.0 for greater durability.
- Turn the tube right side out. Fasturn makes it easy to turn the tubes right side out. For general directions, see page 14.
- Wrap a loop around the button; mark the length using a removable fabric marking pen. Cut the loop ½" beyond the marks. (The loop is approximately 1" longer than the button circumference.) Cut three more loops the same size.

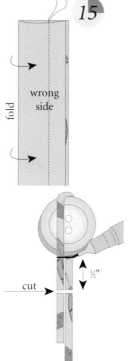

fold

wrong side

cut

½"

Instead of making fabric button loops, you could use any type of elasticized cord as an alternative. For example, there are elasticized gift ties, stretch cords used as hair accessories, as well as elastic cord or thread. Choose whichever you prefer.

Nancy

- Position the button loops on the exterior of the basket 1" from the top edge as shown. Baste in place.

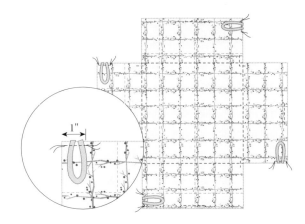

5. Using 2" wide bias strips, prepare approximately 2 yards of bias binding as detailed on page 92.

6. Mark the interior of the basket ½" from each inside and outside corner.

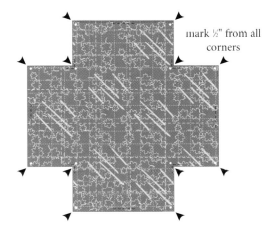

mark ½" from all corners

Position the binding on the interior of the basket; bind the outer edge, following the instructions on page 94 for mitering the outside corners. When you come to an inside corner:

• Stop stitching at the marked point, leaving the needle down in the fabric.
• Gently pivot the fabric under the binding so the second side of the cutout aligns with the edge of the binding. Continue stitching to the next corner mark.

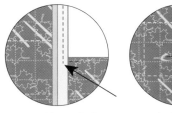

stop with needle in down position

pivot fabric and continue stitching

• Repeat the steps at the remaining corners. Fold the binding to the exterior of the basket and complete the binding as indicated on pages 92-96.

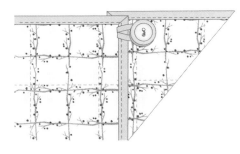

7. Sew buttons to the basket.
• Close the cutout corner, overlapping the corners until the stitched edges of the binding meet. Finger pin and mark inside the loop to indicate the button position.

• Hand stitch the buttons at the markings, adding thread shanks to provide room for the thickness of the thread loop.
• Button the basket corners and you're ready for your guests. After the party, unbutton the buttons, wipe the basket clean, and store it flat.

Add a layer of heat-reflective fabric to the Fold 'n Go Basket for another versatile kitchen accessory with both function and flair. We've included cotton batting and heat-reflective fabric to keep hot dishes hot while at the same time protecting your tabletop. Store the Casserole Cozy flat until you're ready to use it, then fold up the sides, fasten the buttons, and you're ready to go. By using 10, 20, and 30 minute segments of sewing time, the cozy will be ready the next time you have a casserole on your menu. This cozy fits a 9" x 13" baking dish.

MATERIALS NEEDED

- ½ yd. Fabric A
- ½ yd. Fabric B
- ½ yd. Fabric C
- ½ yd. Iron Quick Fabric
- ½ yd. muslin
- ½ yd. cotton batting
- Four ¾" to ⅞" buttons

Fold 'n Go Casserole Cozy

Making the Casserole Cozy

1. Cut out the fabrics. **20**
- Fabric A: Cut one 14" x 18" rectangle (basket exterior).
- Fabric B: Cut five 2" wide bias strips (binding). Cut one ⅞" wide 16" long bias strip (button loops).
- Fabric C: Cut one 14" x 18" rectangle (basket interior).
- Iron Quick: Cut one 14" x 18" rectangle.
- Muslin: Cut one 14" x 18" rectangle (basket lining).
- Cotton batting: Cut two 14" x 18" rectangles. It's important to use cotton batting, since it won't be damaged by the heat from a hot dish, as a synthetic batting might be.

2. Layer and quilt the exterior for the cozy, **20** using the 14" x 18" rectangles of muslin, cotton batting, and Fabric A as detailed on page 90. *Optional:* If the fabric has a natural grid like Fabric A does, follow that grid in quilting. Quilt as many or as few rows as you like.

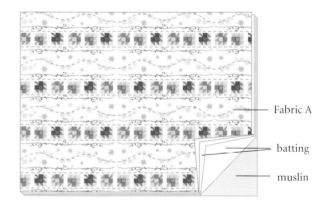

Fabric A

batting

muslin

3. Layer the remaining fabrics. **15**
- Place the quilted fabric, muslin side up.
- Position the Iron Quick, metallic side up, over the muslin.
- Place the Fabric C rectangle over the Iron Quick, right side up.

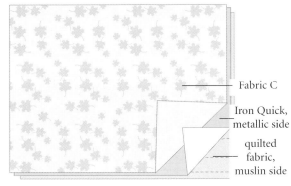

Fabric C

Iron Quick, metallic side

quilted fabric, muslin side

• Baste through all the layers for several inches along the centers of the outer edges, stitching ¼" from the edge.

baste

• Square up the quilt sandwich. Trim away a 2" square from each corner.

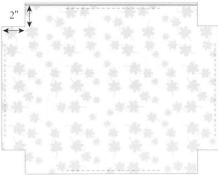

2"

remove 2" corner squares

4. To construct the remainder of the cozy, refer to steps 3 through 7 for the Fold 'n Go Basket, pages 26-27.

Fold 'n Go Bread Basket

Modify the dimensions of the Fold 'n Go Basket to accommodate other items on your menu. For example, a larger 6" x 17" size might be ideal as a bread basket. The construction is the same; only the dimensions change.

MATERIALS NEEDED
- ½ yd. Fabric A
- ½ yd. Fabric B
- ⅓ yd. Fabric C
- ½ yd. Reinforced Plastic
- ½ yd. batting
- Four ¾" to ⅞" buttons

1. Cut out the fabrics.

20

- Fabric A: Cut one 13" x 24" rectangle (basket exterior).
- Fabric B: Cut one 13" x 24" rectangle (basket interior).
- Fabric C: Cut bias strips 2" wide to equal approximately 2½ yards of binding.
  Cut one ⅞" wide 16" long bias strip (button loops).
- Reinforced Plastic: Cut one 13" x 24" rectangle (basket lining).
- Batting: Cut one 13" x 24" rectangle.

2. Shape and construct the basket the same as the Fold 'n Go Basket, removing 3" squares from each of the four corners.

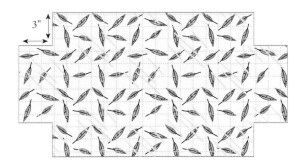

3"

The convenience of the Wrap 'n Go Casserole Carrier will really help you get a handle on things! After you cook up a culinary masterpiece, place the dish in the center, then just wrap and go! The insulated carrier is perfect for picnics or potluck dinners, since it has an additional inner pocket where you can insert a hot or cold pack to keep the temperature of your dish just right. Velcro strips keep your dish nestled safely inside, two side pockets hold serving utensils, and handles make for easy carrying. An added bonus: it stores flat when not in use. What a great gift for a bridal shower, birthday, or housewarming!

MATERIALS NEEDED

- ¾ yd. Fabric A
- ⅜ yd. Fabric B
- ¼ yd. Fabric C
- ¾ yd. quilted Iron Quick Fabric
- ¼ yd. Velcro

Wrap 'n Go Casserole Carrier

Making the Casserole Carrier

1. Cut out the fabrics. **15**
- Iron Quick: Cut two 13" x 36" rectangles (carrier lining).
- Fabric A: Cut two 13" x 36" rectangles (pocket base and handle base).
- Fabric B: Cut one 13" x 44" rectangle (pocket).
- Fabric C: Cut two 4" x 36" rectangles (handles).

2. Make the pocket for the carrier. **5**
- Meet the 13" edges of the Fabric B 13" x 44" pocket, right sides together. Stitch a ¼" seam.
- Press the seam open. Turn the pocket tube right side out, centering the seam, then press.
- Edgestitch the 13" edges.

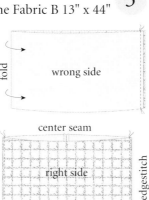

center seam

wrong side

fold

right side

edgestitch

3. Complete the pocket panel of the carrier. **30**
- Fold the Fabric A pocket base in half, meeting the 13" ends; pin mark the fold to indicate the center. Repeat, marking the center of the pocket.
- Position and pin the pocket to the right side of the base, meeting the center marks and raw edges. Baste the pocket to the base ⅛" from the cut edges.

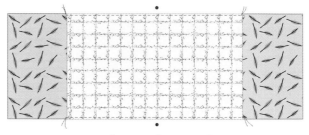

match centers; baste cut edges

- Center and stitch a 5½" loop side section of the Velcro to the right side of one short edge of the base.

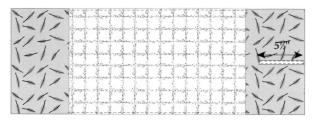

add Velcro loop tape

- Center and stitch a 3" hook side of the Velcro to the reflective side of one short edge of one Iron Quick section.

3" hook tape — Iron Quick, reflective side

- Meet and pin the completed pocket base to the Iron Quick, right sides together, checking to make sure the Velcro sections are at opposite ends. Round all four corners using a Radial Rule or a saucer.

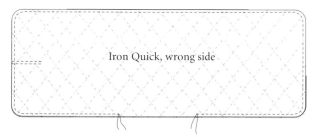

Iron Quick, wrong side

- Stitch a ½" seam around the outer edge, leaving a 6" to 8" opening at the center of one long edge for turning.

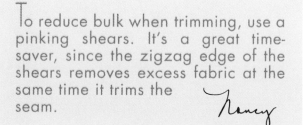

Iron Quick, wrong side

- Press the seams open. Trim the corners.

To reduce bulk when trimming, use a pinking shears. It's a great time-saver, since the zigzag edge of the shears removes excess fabric at the same time it trims the seam. *Nancy*

- Turn the pocket panel right side out. Press the edges. Edgestitch around the outer edge of the panel, stitching the opening closed at the same time.

- Stitch between the lengthwise edges, 6" from each short edge of the panel.

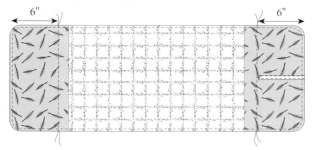

6"   6"

4. Prepare the handle panel of the Casserole Carrier. **20**
- Center and stitch a 3" loop side of the Velcro to the right side of one short edge of the Fabric A handle base.
- Center and stitch a 5½" hook side of the Velcro to the reflective side of one short edge of the remaining Iron Quick section.

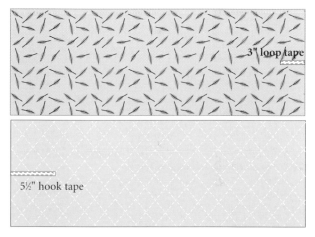

3" loop tape

5½" hook tape

- Join the handle base and Iron Quick section, right sides together, with a ½" seam. Trim, press, turn, and edgestitch as for the pocketed panel.

5. Make handles. **15**
- Meet the 4" edges of the two Fabric C 4" x 36" sections, right sides together. Stitch ½" seams at each end. Press the seams open.

meet right sides; stitch

- Meet the lengthwise edges of the handle, wrong sides together. Press fold.

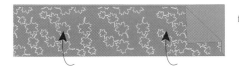

fold, wrong sides together

- Unfold the handle and meet the cut edges to the center press mark, wrong sides together. Press.

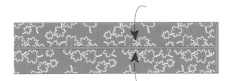

meet cut edges to fold

- Fold again, meeting the folded edges; press. Edgestitch both edges of the handle.

6. Attach the handles to the handle panel. **20**
- Fold the handle base in half, meeting the short ends. Mark the center.
- Position the handle on the handle base, 3" from each lengthwise edge, meeting the handle seams to the base center marks. Pin the handle in place.

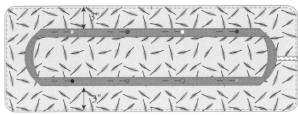

match seams to centers; pin handles

- Measure 6" from each short edge. Mark from lengthwise edge to lengthwise edge. This indicates starting and stopping points for stitching the handles.
- Edgestitch each side of both handle strips between the 6" markings.

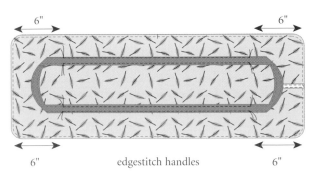

6"   6"

6"   edgestitch handles   6"

- Stitch from edge to edge along the marked 6" line.

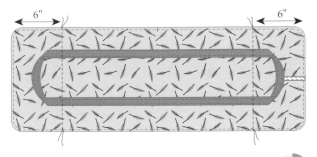

6"   6"

7. Join the carrier panels. **10**
- Place the pocket panel, fabric side up. Mark the center of the pocket.
- Meet the short ends of the handle panel; mark the center.
- Place the handle panel at a right angle to the pocket panel, fabric side up, meeting the center marks. The handle panel will be approximately 11½" from the ends of the pocket panel. Pin in place.
- Stitch along three sides to secure the layers, leaving the fourth side open for inserting a hot or cold pack.

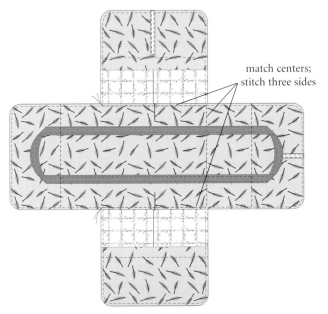

match centers; stitch three sides

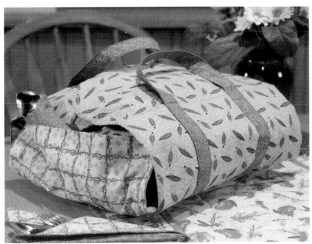

Fast-Patch Table Runner

Now that you have some attractive food containers for your table, let's take a look at the table itself.

This attractive table runner is designed to showcase your favorite fabrics. We used four coordinates, including a patchwork bird print. The simple design and bias trim highlight each fabric.

Creating the table runner is easy. Just place fabric pieces down flat, then join them with bias tape you make yourself. With the simple flat patchwork technique, in no time flat you can create an attractive table accent.

FINISHED SIZE
Approximately 18" x 44"

MATERIALS NEEDED
- ⅝ yd. Fabric A
- ½ yd. Fabric B
- ⅛ yd. Fabric C
- ⅓ yd. Fabric D
- ⅝ yd. Fabric E
- ⅝ yd. batting

Making the Table Runner

1. Cut out the fabrics.
   - Fabric A: Cut two 3½" x 11" rectangles (left and right borders).
   - Cut two 3½" x 37" rectangles (top and bottom borders).
   - Fabric B: Cut one 11" x 37" rectangle (table runner center).
   - Fabric C: Cut eight 3½" squares (corner blocks).
   - Fabric D: Cut five ¾" wide crosswise strips (sashing strips).
     Cut three 1½" wide crosswise strips (binding).
   - Fabric E: Cut one 21" x 44" rectangle (backing).
   - Batting: Cut one 21" x 44" rectangle.

10

We used a printed fabric containing blocks of birds for the borders on our table runner. When using novelty prints, sometimes the design of the fabric itself gives an indication of how big to cut the individual pattern pieces. For example, we cut border rectangles so the patchwork birds were centered between the short ends of the rectangles. We cut the upper edge of each rectangle approximately ⅜" above the twig frames, and we cut the lower edge of each rectangle approximately ⅝" below the twig frames.

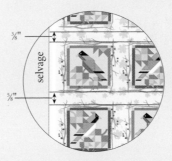

Nancy

2. Prepare fusible sashing strips.
- Insert ¾" Fabric D strips, wrong side up, into the lower opening of the ⅜" Fusible Bias Tape Maker.
- Insert ¼" paper-backed fusible tape into the top slot.
- Gently pull the handle of the tape maker as you press the folded fabric.

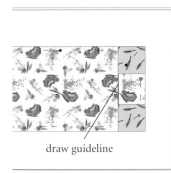

paper-backed fusible web

3. Flat-patch the center of the table runner.

- Place the backing fabric on a flat surface, wrong side up.
- Place the batting over the backing.
- Position the Fabric B table runner center over the batting, right side up. Pin the layers in place.

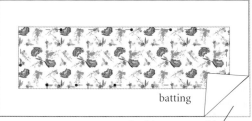

batting

backing, wrong side

- Position the Fabric C squares over the four corners of the Fabric B center rectangle, aligning the cut edges. Pin in place.

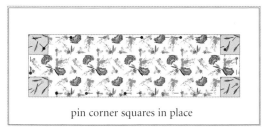

pin corner squares in place

- Draw a guideline between the interior corners of the squares on one end of the table runner. Repeat on the opposite end.

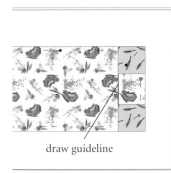

draw guideline

- Cut and position 3½" fusible sashing strips to cover the inner cut edges of the squares, extending from the outer cut edge to the drawn guideline. Fuse.

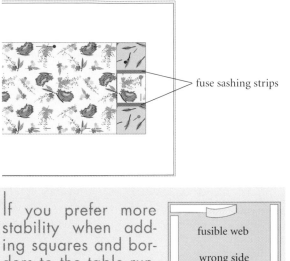

fuse sashing strips

If you prefer more stability when adding squares and borders to the table runner, press ⅜" strips of paper-backed fusible web along the outer edges of the wrong side of each section. Remove the paper backing from the tape, position the sections over the base, and press the sections in place. Nancy

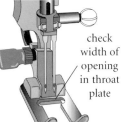

fusible web

wrong side

- Attach an Open Toe Foot. The open front of this foot makes it easier to see exactly where you're stitching. Stitch along each edge of the strips with a straight stitch. Or use a double needle to stitch both edges of the tape at the same time. Use a 4.0 double needle with ¼" tape, and a 6.0 double needle with ⅜" tape.
  - Make certain the opening in the sewing machine throat plate is wide enough to accommodate the needle so you don't break the needle or damage the throat plate.

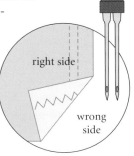

check width of opening in throat plate

  - You can use a double needle on any zigzag sewing machine that threads from front to back. A double needle makes two parallel lines of stitching on the right side of the fabric, while on the wrong side a single bobbin thread moves back and forth between the two needle threads, resembling a zigzag.

right side

wrong side

When using a double needle, you need two threads on top of the machine. I like to position one so it unwinds clockwise, and the other, counterclockwise. Thread the two top threads through the machine as if they were a single thread, separating them at the needle and inserting one through each needle. Slightly loosening the needle tension by one or two numbers helps prevent tunneling. *Nancy*

• Position an 11" fusible sashing strip along the inner edges of the corner squares at each end of the table runner, following the guidelines and covering the cut edges of the squares and the ends of first sashing strips. Fuse. Stitch the strips in place.

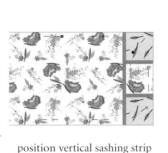

position vertical sashing strip

4. Add the top, bottom, and end borders. **10**
• Butt the long cut edges of the 3½" x 37" Fabric A border to the top and bottom edges of the table runner. Pin in place.

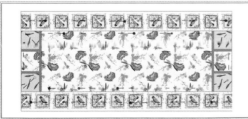

add top and bottom borders

• Position and butt the cut edges of the 3½" Fabric C corner squares and the 3½" x 11" Fabric A left and right borders to the left and right edges of the table runner. Pin in place.

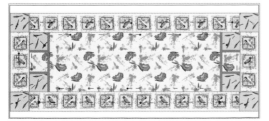

add corner squares and side borders

5. Cover the inner edges of the table runner borders with fusible sashing strips. **15**
• Center the sashing strips over the butted top and bottom border edges, covering all the raw edges. Fuse and stitch the strips in place.

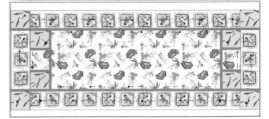

• Center, fuse, and stitch the sashing strips over the butted left and right border cut edges.

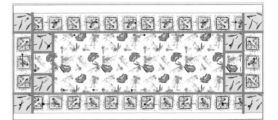

6. Quilt the table runner as detailed on page 90, stitching along both sides of each fusible sashing strip. **30**

• *Optional:* Quilt the center of the table runner. For ease in quilting, if the fabrics have a natural grid, follow that grid when doing the quilting.

stitch along all sashing strips

• Trim the backing and batting even with the table runner. Square the runner and machine baste ¼" from the edges.

7. Prepare ¾" bias tape using a ¾" Bias Tape Maker as detailed on page 92. **10**

8. Bind the edges of the table runner, mitering the corners as detailed on pages 92-96. **30**

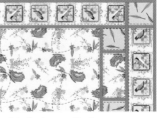

bind edges, mitering corners

Give your table settings a facelift with these attractive placemats and coasters. Woven fabric tubes give them a character all their own. This project is a great way to use fabric remnants. The only requirement is that pieces must be at least 18" long.

Using a Fasturn makes it easy to create and turn the tubes needed for this project. Then simply weave strips of coordinating colors to get precisely the look you want.

FINISHED SIZE

Approximately 13" x 17"

MATERIALS NEEDED

(Makes two placemats and coasters)

- Approximately 2 yd. assorted coordinating fabrics
- ½ yd. binding fabric
- 1 yd. 45" wide batting

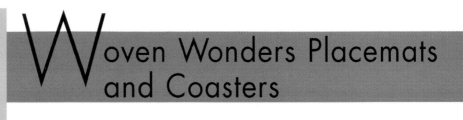

Woven Wonders Placemats and Coasters

Making the Placemats

1. Cut out the fabric pieces.
- Coordinating fabrics: Cut several 18" long *20* strips of the following widths: 2", 3½", and 5½".
- Binding fabric: Cut 2" wide bias strips to equal approximately 4¾ yards of binding.
- Batting: Cut strips of the following widths: ¾", 1½", and 2½", to correlate with the fabric strips.

2. Stitch and stuff the fabric tubes.
- Stitch all the strips into tubes, right sides together, using ¼" seams.

30

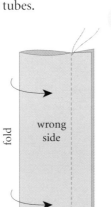

fold

wrong side

- Place the stitched tube over the appropriate Fasturn cylinder. (We used sizes #4, #5, and #6.) Press the seams open.

For quick pressing, use the Fasturn cylinder as a pressing surface. Just run your fingernail or a wooden pressing tool like the Little Wooden Iron along the opened seam. *Nancy*

- Wrap the fabric over the end of the cylinder. Insert the hook and turn clockwise to secure the hook.

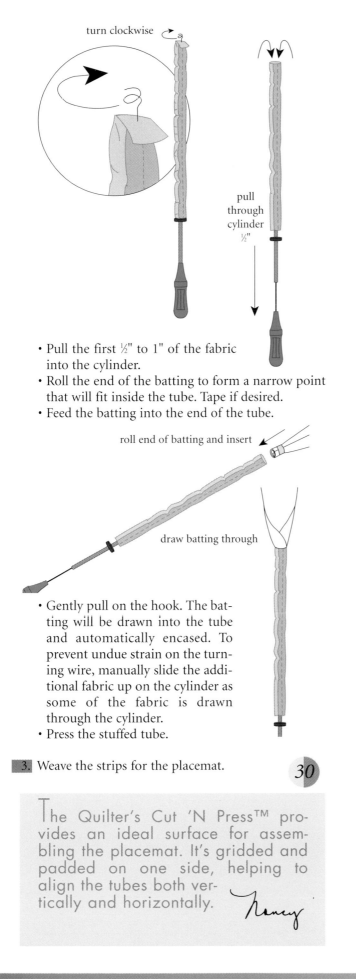

turn clockwise

pull
through
cylinder
½"

- Pull the first ½" to 1" of the fabric into the cylinder.
- Roll the end of the batting to form a narrow point that will fit inside the tube. Tape if desired.
- Feed the batting into the end of the tube.

roll end of batting and insert

draw batting through

- Gently pull on the hook. The batting will be drawn into the tube and automatically encased. To prevent undue strain on the turning wire, manually slide the additional fabric up on the cylinder as some of the fabric is drawn through the cylinder.
- Press the stuffed tube.

3. Weave the strips for the placemat. ③⓪

The Quilter's Cut 'N Press™ provides an ideal surface for assembling the placemat. It's gridded and padded on one side, helping to align the tubes both vertically and horizontally. *Nancy*

- Pin the top and bottom of the assorted sizes and colorations of stuffed tubes to a padded surface to measure 17" to 18" across, butting the edges.

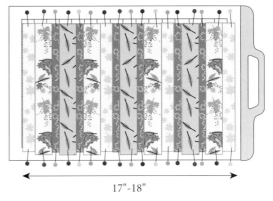

17"-18"

- Weave the horizontal strips snugly to form a "quilted" fabric approximately 13" to 14" high, arranging the sizes and colorations of the strips to make a pleasing arrangement. Pin baste the layers together along the outside edges.

13"–14"

- Round the corners. Machine baste ¼" from the edge, removing the pins as you come to them.

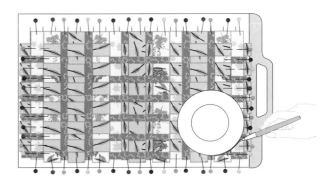

4. Weave coasters following the same process, weaving a stuffed quilted fabric section approximately 6" square. Cut 5" circles, machine basting ¼" from the outer edge. ①⑤

5. Prepare approximately 4¾ yd. binding as detailed on page 92. ①⑤

6. Bind the edges of the placemats and coasters as detailed on pages 92-96. ③⓪

Complete your table setting with these reversible napkins. Use a variety of coordinating fabrics and a simple self-fabric binding for fun mix-n-match possibilities. In less than an hour's sewing time, you can make a set of four napkins. Fold the napkins, and they're ready to add zest and style to your next gathering.

FINISHED SIZE

Approximately 16" square

MATERIALS NEEDED

- ½ yd. Fabric A
- 1 yd. Fabric B
- ½ yd. Fabric C

Making the Napkins

1. Cut the fabrics.
   - Fabric A: Cut two 16" squares.
   - Fabric B: Cut four 18" squares.
   - Fabric C: Cut two 16" squares.

10

2. Prepare the napkin layers.
   - Trim the corners of the large Fabric B napkin squares.
     - Mark 1" from each side of each corner.

15

mark 1" from all corners

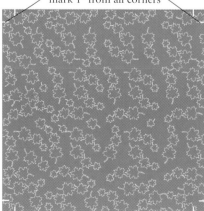

- Draw a diagonal line across each corner, connecting the marks.

draw diagonal lines to connect marks

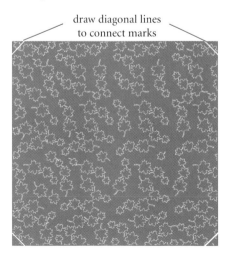

- Cut away the small triangle formed by the drawn line.

trim corners

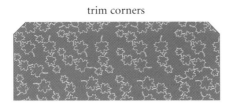

- Place the napkin square wrong side up.
- Center the small napkin square over the large square, right side up. The large square should extend beyond the small square 1" on all sides.

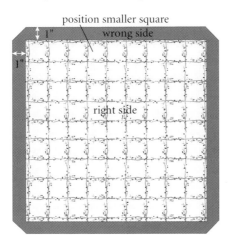

position smaller square

1"

wrong side

1"

right side

- Fold in the trimmed corners of the large square ½" to cover the corners of the small square. Press.

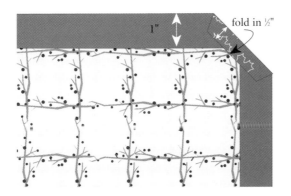

1"

fold in ½"

- Press the cut edges of the large square to meet the edges of the small square.

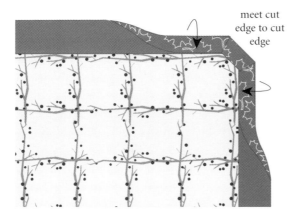

meet cut edge to cut edge

- Fold the pressed edge over the small square a second time, encasing all the cut edges and creating a ½" "binding" with mitered corners.
- Pin along the binding to secure the layers and prevent shifting.

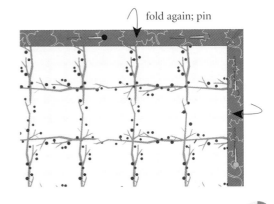

fold again; pin

3. Edgestitch the napkin edges, removing the pins as you come to them. Stitch along the inside fold of the binding, sewing into the corners to secure the miters.

5

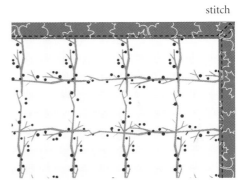

stitch

If you use solid colored fabrics for making napkins, consider edge-stitching with one of your sewing machine decorative stitches. For example, try a feather stitch. This step takes slightly longer, yet the results are definitely worthwhile.

Nancy

Transform an ordinary basket into an attractive home accent in mere minutes with this simple to sew or serge project. Choose and join two coordinating fabrics, add an elastic casing, and you're finished. You'll want garters for every season and holiday. And what a great gift!

MATERIALS NEEDED

- Two coordinating fabrics
- ⅜" elastic
- Narrow strips of paper-backed fusible web

Note: *Amounts needed will vary, depending on the size of the basket.*

Basket Garter

Making the Basket Garter

1. Determine the garter dimensions and cut out **10** the fabrics.
   - Measure the basket height. Add ½" for seam allowances.
   - Measure the basket circumference; multiply by 2.5.

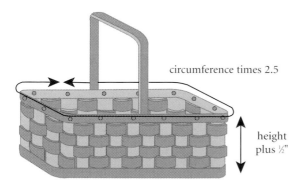

circumference times 2.5

height plus ½"

   - Cut crosswise strips of two coordinating fabrics, using the height measurement plus ½". Cut as many strips as needed to achieve the desired circumference. It's not necessary to trim the strips to

the precise length. Extra inches give additional fullness and make the garter even more attractive. Here's a guideline:
   - Small basket: Cut one strip of each fabric.
   - Medium basket: Cut two strips of each fabric.
   - Large basket: Cut three strips of each fabric.

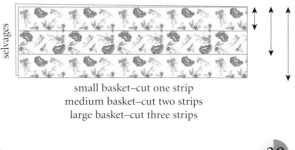

selvages

small basket–cut one strip
medium basket–cut two strips
large basket–cut three strips

2. Completing the garter using a sewing **30** machine:
   - Join strips of one fabric into a long strip, right sides together, using a narrow seam allowance. Press the seam(s) open. Repeat for the second fabric.

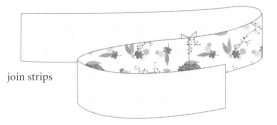

join strips

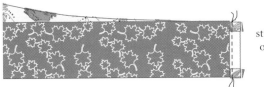

stitch ends of longer strips

• Fuse the seam allowances in the pressed position, using a narrow strip of fusible web. This makes it easier to insert the elastic.

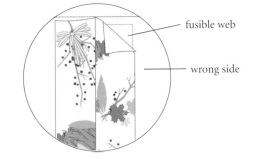

fusible web

wrong side

• Press under ½" along both short ends of one of the strips.

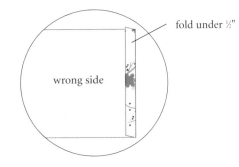

fold under ½"

wrong side

• Pin the strips, right sides together, with the longer strip extending ½" at each end. Stitch ¼" seams along the top and bottom edges.

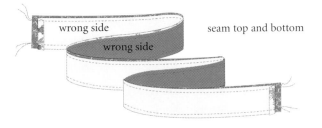

wrong side

wrong side

seam top and bottom

• Press the seams flat, then press them open.
• Turn the garter right side out; press.
• Meet the unsewn ends, right sides together, to form a circle. Stitch a ½" seam, taking care not to catch the edges of the shorter strip. Press the seam open.

• Tuck the stitched seam allowances inside the tube.
• Meet the lengthwise edges of the garter; press to mark the center.
• Unfold the garter; stitch ¼" on either side of the fold mark to form the casing.

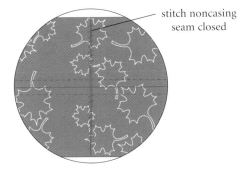

stitch ¼" on each side of fold mark

• Hand stitch closed all except the casing portion of the seam.

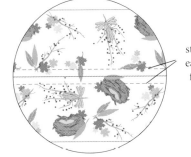

stitch noncasing seam closed

3. Completing the garter using a serger:
  • Join the short ends of the Fabric A strips to form a circle, right sides together, using narrow seam allowances. (You may prefer to use a sewing machine for this step.)
  • Repeat for the Fabric B strips, leaving a ½" opening in the middle of one seam to provide room for inserting the elastic.
  • Meet the circles, wrong sides together, matching the seamlines.

20

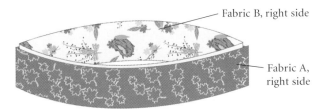

Fabric B, right side

Fabric A, right side

- Adjust your serger for a rolled edge. Use these general guidelines. Check the owner's manual for more detailed instructions.
  - Remove the left needle.
  - Attach the rolled edge plate or foot.
  - Tighten the lower looper.
  - Loosen the upper looper.
  - Thread the upper looper with a specialty serging thread. For example, use Woolly Nylon to help fill out the seam or choose a decorative thread to add luster and sheen.
  - Use all-purpose serging thread that matches the fabric in the needle and lower looper.
  - Test stitch on a fabric scrap; adjust tensions or threads as necessary.
- Serge both the lengthwise edges of the stacked circles.
  - Cut a "starting gate" along each lengthwise edge by cutting out a ¼" x 1" section.
  - Place the serger foot in the starting gate, aligning the blade area next to the cutout section.

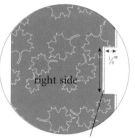

cut starting gate

align foot and serger blade next to cutout section

- Serge along the edge, trimming off the ¼" seam allowance. (The stitch quality is generally improved if a small amount of fabric is trimmed away, rather than serging precisely along the cut edge.)
- At the end of the serging, serge over several of the beginning stitches to secure the threads. Release the threads from the stitch finger and clip the threads.
- Apply Fray Check™ to the thread ends to secure them. After the Fray Check is dry, clip the thread tails close to the stitching.

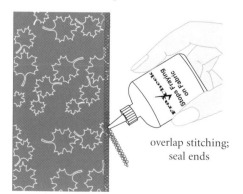

overlap stitching; seal ends

- Use a sewing machine to stitch the casing, following the technique above.

4. Insert the elastic in the casing.
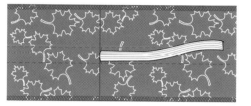

10

- Cut a length of ⅜" elastic 2" shorter than the circumference of the basket.
- Insert the elastic through the casing with a bodkin or the String Thing.

insert ⅜" elastic

The String Thing makes it easy to thread elastic through casings, especially long casings like that on the Basket Garter. Loop the elastic through the eye at the end of the String Thing. Then insert the String Thing in the casing and pull the elastic through. It's as easy as that!

Nancy

- Butt the elastic ends over a fabric scrap. Stitch elastic to the fabric scrap to join the ends. Trim the excess fabric.

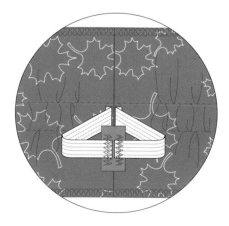

Sewing for Easy, Casual Living

A beautiful summer day is the perfect time to get out of the house and enjoy a picnic in the park. Here are two projects designed for your "home away from home" on those days. This tote bag is large enough to hold all of your picnic supplies, with handy pockets for storing silverware and plates or a Frisbee for after-dinner entertainment. The wine tote is a perfect complement. So sit back, relax, and enjoy!

FINISHED SIZE
Tote bag
6½"W x 24"L x 14½"H
Wine tote
8"W x 2½"D x 15"H

MATERIALS NEEDED
(makes both totes)
- ¾ yd. oilcloth Fabric A
- ¼ yd. oilcloth B
- ½ yd. oilcloth C
- 1⅛ yd. oilcloth D
- 3 yd. cotton webbing

Note: *All seam allowances are ¼".*

On-the-Go Picnic Totes

Making the Tote Bag

1. Cut out the fabrics for the tote bag and wine tote. *15*
   - **Oilcloth A:**
     - Cut two 15" x 24" rectangles (tote bag front and back).
     - Cut two 5" x 6" rectangles (tote bag side pockets).
     - Cut one 10" x 32" rectangle (wine tote).

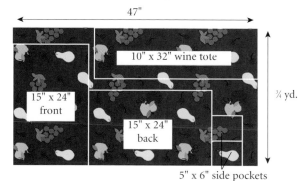

47"

10" x 32" wine tote

15" x 24" front

15" x 24" back

¾ yd.

5" x 6" side pockets

   - **Oilcloth B:**
     - Cut two 8" x 14" rectangles (bag center pockets).
     - Cut one 7" x 9½" rectangle (wine tote pocket).
   - **Oilcloth C:** Cut two 7" x 27½" strips (bag sides/base).

   - **Oilcloth D:**
     - Cut two 7" x 27½" strips (bag side and base lining).
     - Cut two 15" x 24" rectangles (bag lining).
     - Cut four 5" x 8" rectangles (bag front/back pockets). For a fun option, cut pockets on the diagonal, giving them the look of bias.
     - Cut one 10" x 32" rectangle (wine tote lining).

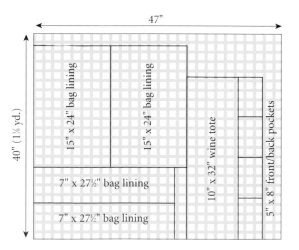

47"

40" (1⅛ yd.)

15" x 24" bag lining

15" x 24" bag lining

10" x 32" wine tote

5" x 8" front/back pockets

7" x 27½" bag lining

7" x 27½" bag lining

2. Set up the sewing machine. **5**
   - Use the standard sewing machine presser foot or a Teflon™ foot. The smooth, Teflon-coated foot glides over hard-to-sew fabrics like oilcloth, preventing the fabric from tugging and pulling against the foot.
   - Use a size 80 Sharp needle.
   - Thread the top and bobbin of the machine with clear monofilament thread. Or thread the bobbin with coordinating all-purpose thread.

3. Add pockets to the Fabric C side/base strip. **15**
   - Scallop the 5" top edge of each Fabric A side pocket.
   - Seam the two Fabric C strips, right sides together, meeting the short ends.
   - Position the scalloped edge of a pocket approximately 6" from each short end of the side/base strip, centering the pockets on the strip. Tape the pockets in place with Sewer's Fix-it Tape.

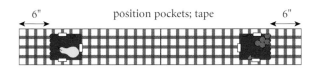

6"   position pockets; tape   6"

   - Edgestitch along the straight edges of the pockets, removing the tape as you come to it.

4. Add the pockets to the bag front and back panels. **20**
   - Scallop the 5" top edge of each Fabric D front/back pocket.
   - Scallop the 14" top edge of both Fabric B center pockets.
   - Position a Fabric D pocket in each lower corner of the bag front. Tape them in place along the scalloped edges.
   - Position a Fabric B pocket between the Fabric D pockets. Tape it in place; machine baste all three pockets in place, stitching close to the cut edges.
   - Repeat, adding pockets to the bag back.

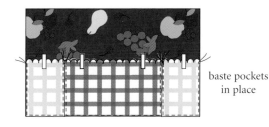

baste pockets in place

5. Add the handles. **10**
   - Cut the webbing into two equal lengths.
   - Center one length over the basted edges of the front pockets, aligning the cut ends with the lower edge of the tote front.
   - Edgestitch the handle, stopping 2" from the top edge.
   - Repeat for the tote back.

edgestitch straps, stopping 2" from upper edge

6. Assemble the tote bag. **10**
   - Mark the seam allowances at both the lower corners with a pencil.
   - Use the edge of the presser foot as a stitching guide when stitching the seams.
   - Roughly center the side/base strip around the tote front, right sides together. Secure the edges for stitching.

Pin marks are permanent in oilcloth, so Binding and Hem Clips are a good "pinning" substitute. They firmly hold the edges in place, yet they leave no marks on the fabric when they're removed.

Nancy

   - With the edges aligned, place the side/base strip next to the machine bed, and begin stitching at the upper corner of the tote front, removing the clips as you sew. Stitch to the marked seamline, stopping with the needle down in the fabric.

seamline

stop with needle down

   - Raise the presser foot and nip the side/base strip perpendicular to the fabric edge, almost to the seamline.

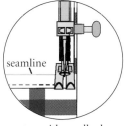

wrong side

right side

nip base strip

- Pivot the tote front, again aligning the lower edge of the tote with the side/base strip. Repeat at the second corner.
- Attach the back to the tote, following the same technique.

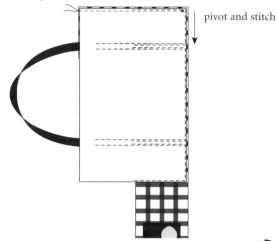

pivot and stitch

7. Seam the tote lining.

10

- Seam the two 27½" Fabric D strips, right sides together, meeting the short ends.
- *Optional:* Add additional pockets to the right sides of the front and back tote linings as detailed for the tote.
- Assemble the lining in the same manner as the tote.

8. Finish the tote bag.

15

- Slip the lining into the tote bag, wrong sides together, matching the seams and aligning the top edges. "Pin" the layers together using binding and hem clips.

- Stitch around the top edge at least ¼" from the cut edges.

pin layers together; stitch around top

- Scallop both layers, being careful not to cut through the stitching.
- Tape the web handles up to the scalloped edge of the tote. Edgestitch along the webbing, reinforcing the stitching as shown.

reinforce straps

Here's another carrier that comes in handy when you have a picnic on your mind. Nestle a bottle of wine in the tote, slip a wine opener in the pocket, and you're ready to go. Or use the tote to carry catsup and other condiments.

Making the Wine Tote

1. Create a pattern.

5

- Fold a length of Pattern Paper in half, meeting the lengthwise edges.
- Follow the illustration to shape the pattern. Use a Styling Design Ruler or a comparably curved ruler to connect the 1½" and 9" marks.
- At the side seam, draw a ¼" line perpendicular to the seam to provide room for a seam allowance.

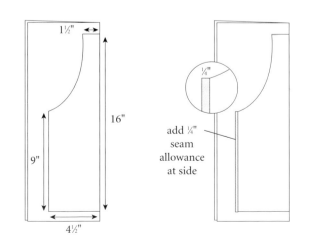

1½"

16"

9"

4½"

¼"

add ¼" seam allowance at side

- Cut out and unfold the pattern. Write "place on fold" on the handle end (the shorter end).

2. Lay out the pattern.
   - Fold the wine tote oilcloth fabric rectangles in half, meeting the 10" edges.
   - Position the pattern on Fabric A oilcloth as shown; cut out the pattern for the tote.

   - Repeat on the Fabric D oilcloth for the lining.

3. Add the pocket.
   - Fold over ½" on the 9½" top edge of the Fabric B pocket and topstitch ¼" from the fold.
   - *Optional:* Scallop the hemmed pocket edge.
   - Position the pocket on the Fabric A wine tote base, meeting the cut edges. Tape the pocket in place along the top edge using small pieces of Sewer's Fix-it Tape. Use Binding and Hem Clips to secure the sides. Machine baste the pocket in place, stitching close to the cut edges and removing the clips as you come to them.

baste pocket in place

4. Stitch the wine tote.
   - Meet the tote pieces, wrong sides together.
   - Stitch the pieces together.
     - Starting at the cut edge, stitch a ¼" straight line, pivot, stitch along the curve, pivot, and stitch a straight line to the cut edge.

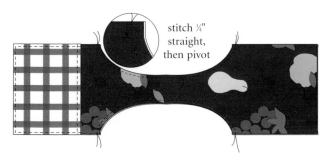

stitch ¼" straight, then pivot

- Make a ¼" clip in the seam allowance at the pivot point, being careful not to cut through the stitching. *Optional:* Trim the seam allowance between the clip and the cut edge.

- Scallop both layers along the curve, cutting even with the stitching line, but being careful not to cut through the stitching.
- Meet the tote pieces, right sides together. Using hem binding clips or paper clips, "pin" and stitch the corresponding side seams of both the Fabric D lining and the Fabric A oilcloth wine totes, matching the seam intersections.

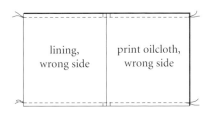

lining, wrong side | print oilcloth, wrong side

- Turn the tote so the Fabric D lining side is out.
- Meet the lower edges, with the right sides of the Fabric A oilcloth together. Stitch through all layers.

stitch lower edge

- Form a gusset at the lower edge.
  - At each corner, fold the fabric so the side seam stacks on top of the lower edge seam, forming a triangle.
  - Use a Radial Rule or a saucer to draw in a slight curve as shown. This makes the tote conform to the shape of a bottle.
  - Stitch along the curve. Repeat on the opposite corner.

2½"   1¼"

- Gather all your picnic supplies, load your new tote bag and wine tote, and head for the woods, the park, or the beach!

Placemats are ideal table coverings for a picnic or a casual lunch on the deck or patio. We offer two variations: one is a simple stitched and scalloped roll-up version with pockets for utensils, while the other is a basic bias-bound mat. Both are easy-sew, and using oilcloth makes cleanup a breeze.

FINISHED SIZE

Approximately 15" x 18"

SCALLOPED-EDGE ROLL-UP PLACEMAT

Your silverware has a home all its own with these pocketed placemats. When the mats aren't in use, roll them up and tie the ribbon ties for easy storage in minimal space.

MATERIALS NEEDED

(makes four placemats)
- 1½ yd. oilcloth Fabric A, or 1 yd. each of two coordinating fabrics
- ¼ yd. oilcloth Fabric B
- 4 yd. ¼" wide grosgrain ribbon

Picture-Perfect Placemats

Making the Scalloped-Edge Placemat

1. Cut out the fabric pieces.
   - Oilcloth Fabric A: Cut eight 15" x 18" rectangles. Or cut four each of two coordinating oilcloth fabrics (placemat bases).
   - Oilcloth Fabric B: Cut four 6" squares (pockets).
   - Grosgrain ribbon: Cut four one yard pieces (ties).

2. Set up the sewing machine.
   - Use the standard sewing machine presser foot or a Teflon foot. The smooth, Teflon-coated foot glides over hard-to-sew fabrics such as oilcloth, preventing the fabric from tugging and pulling against the foot.
   - Use a size 80 Sharp needle.
   - Thread the top and bobbin of the machine with clear monofilament thread. Or use coordinating all-purpose thread in the bobbin.

3. Trim three edges of each pocket, using a scallop scissors or pinking shears to add a decorative finish.

scallop three sides

4. Assemble the placemats.
   - Position the pocket 2" away from the short edge of one base rectangle, aligning the unscalloped edges. Secure with Sewer's Fix-it Tape. This tape temporarily secures the pocket, yet can be easily removed without leaving residue.
   - Stitch the left and right edges in place. Divide the pocket into three smaller sections by stitching vertical lines 2" apart.

position pocket; stitch vertical seams

2"

- Meet the 15" x 18" rectangles, wrong sides together. "Pin" with Binding and Hem Clips or paper clips to avoid visible pinholes.
- Edgestitch ¼" from the edges of the placemat.

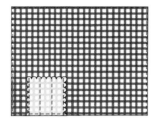

edgestitch
placemat

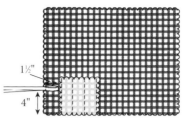

1½"

4"

- Place silverware in the pocket sections.
- Fold the placemat in half, meeting the 18" edges.

5. Finish the placemat.
   - Trim the outer edges of the placemat with a scallop scissors, cutting through all layers.
   - Fold the tie in half. Position the ribbon on the placemat, placing the fold 1½" from the left edge and 4" above the bottom edge. Stitch the end of the ribbon in place.

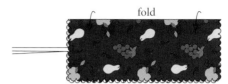

fold

- Roll up the placemat, beginning with the end opposite the ties. Wrap the ties around the rolled mat. Tie the ends to secure the mat.

Here's another placemat option. Start with two layers of oilcloth. Bind the edges, and you're definitely ready for that picnic in the park.

MATERIALS NEEDED

(makes four placemats)
- 1½ yd. oilcloth fabric
- ½ yd. woven fabric for binding

Making the Bound-Edge Placemat

3. Assemble the placemat.
   - Meet the two rectangles wrong sides together. Secure the layers with Binding and Hem Clips.
   - *Optional:* Round the corners using a Radial Rule or a saucer.
   - Edgestitch ¼" from the outer edges, removing the clips as you come to them.

4. Prepare the binding as detailed on page 92. (Each placemat requires approximately 72" of binding.)

5. Bind the placemat as detailed on pages 92-96.

1. Cut out the fabric pieces.
   - Oilcloth: Cut eight 15" x 18" rectangles (placemat bases).
   - Binding: Cut 2" wide bias strips to equal approximately eight to nine yards of binding.

2. Set up the sewing machine as detailed for the Scalloped-Edge Placemat (page 48).

Give an ordinary folding chair a facelift with these oil-cloth Chair Back Covers. An optional Velcro closure helps keep the cover in place, while perky bows, also optional, help transform the chair and its cover into the best seat in the house.

FINISHED SIZE

Approximately 9" x 19½"

MATERIALS NEEDED

(makes two covers)
- ⅔ yd. oilcloth fabric
- 8" of 1" wide grosgrain ribbon for reinforcement
- 2" strip Velcro for closure

Chair Back Cover

Making the Chair Back Cover

1. Cut out the fabric pieces.
   - Oilcloth: Cut one 20" square for each chair back cover.
   - *Optional:* Cut the fabrics for the closure.
     - Grosgrain ribbon: Cut two 2" strips for each cover.
     - Velcro: Cut a 1" strip for each cover.
   - *Optional:* Cut the oilcloth fabric for the bows.
     - Cut four 4" x 6" rectangles (bows).
     - Cut two 2" x 4" rectangles (ties).

2. Set up the sewing machine as detailed in Step 2 for the Scalloped-Edge Roll-Up Placemat, page 48.

3. *Optional:* Add a Velcro closure to secure the cover to the chair.
   - Fold each strip of grosgrain ribbon in half, meeting the cut edges. Center the folded ribbons on the right side of the opposite edges of the oilcloth, meeting the cut edges of the ribbon to those of the chair cover. Secure with Sewer's Fix-it Tape.

- Place a 1" strip of hook tape over the ribbon at one edge of the cover. Place a 1" strip of loop tape over the ribbon at the opposite edge. Stitch the Velcro in place, stitching through all the layers.

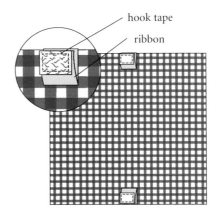

hook tape

ribbon

4. *Optional:* Add appliqués.
   - Carefully cut out the motifs from a contrasting oilcloth print.
   - Use Sewer's Fix-it Tape to position the appliqués 2" from the cut edge of one of the edges of the cover.

(If the cover includes a Velcro closure, place the appliqués along one of those edges.) Stitch the appliqués in place, removing the tape as you come to it.

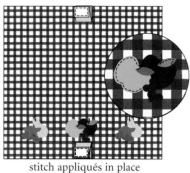

stitch appliqués in place

This is a super-quick way to add an appliqué to a project. Because oilcloth doesn't ravel, you don't have to worry about zigzagging or finishing the edges of the appliqués. Use this same technique to add no-ravel appliqués to other projects such as placemats, totes, and lunch bags. You're limited only by your imagination.

Nancy

5. Assemble the chair cover. **10**
   • Fold the oilcloth square in half, right sides together, meeting the edges with the Velcro closures. Stitch the side seams.

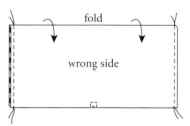

fold over ½"

• Turn up a 1" hem. Secure the hem with Binding and Hem Clips. Stitch the hem, removing the clips as you come to them.

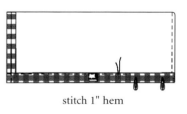

stitch 1" hem

6. *Optional:* Add oilcloth bows. **15**
   • Meet two 4" x 6" rectangles, wrong sides together. Secure with Binding and Hem Clips. Stitch ¼" from all the edges, removing the clips as you come to them.
   • Scallop the edges.

• Fold over ½" on one 6" edge. Accordion pleat the remainder of the rectangle, alternately folding the edge toward the front and then toward the back.

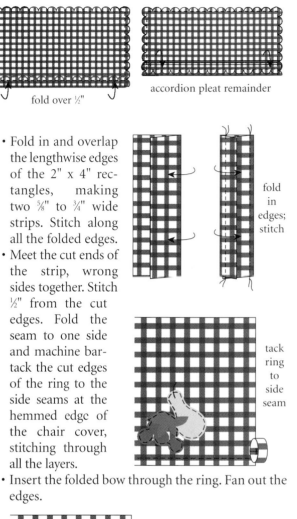

fold over ½" accordion pleat remainder

• Fold in and overlap the lengthwise edges of the 2" x 4" rectangles, making two ⅝" to ¾" wide strips. Stitch along all the folded edges.

fold in edges; stitch

• Meet the cut ends of the strip, wrong sides together. Stitch ½" from the cut edges. Fold the seam to one side and machine bartack the cut edges of the ring to the side seams at the hemmed edge of the chair cover, stitching through all the layers.

tack ring to side seam

• Insert the folded bow through the ring. Fan out the edges.

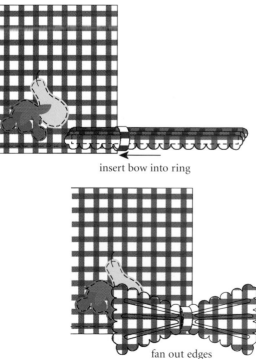

insert bow into ring

fan out edges

When you're brown-bagging it, carry your lunch with you in style with this attractive lunch bag. It wipes clean with a damp cloth and the sewing is "sew" easy. Pack the bag full of goodies for a homemade lunch on the go!

FINISHED SIZE

Approximately
6½" x 9" x 4½" deep

MATERIALS NEEDED

- ¼ yd. oilcloth Fabric A
- ¼ yd. oilcloth Fabric B
- *Optional:* 2" strip Velcro for closure

Lunch-on-the-Go Bag

Making the Lunch Bag

1. Cut out the fabric pieces. **10**
   - Oilcloth Fabric A: Cut two 7" x 11" rectangles (front and back).
   - Oilcloth Fabric B: Cut one 5" x 29" strip (sides and base).

2. Set up the sewing machine as detailed in Step 2 for the Scalloped-Edge Roll-Up Placemat, page 48. **5**

3. Assemble the lunch bag. **20**
   - *Optional:* Add a Velcro closure to the bag.
     - Center the hook side of a 2" strip of Velcro on the right side of the back oilcloth section, ¾" from the top. Stitch the outer edges in place.
     - Center the loop side of the 2" strip of Velcro on the right side of the front oilcloth section, 2½" from the top. Stitch in place.

position hook tape on back section   position loop tape on front section

- Mark ¼" from the lower corners of the front and back.

mark ¼" from corners

- Meet the lengthwise edges of the front and the 5" x 29" strip, wrong sides together, placing the side/base on the bottom.
- Stitch, stopping at the corner marking with the needle down to secure the oilcloth.

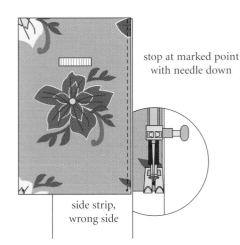

stop at marked point with needle down

side strip, wrong side

- Clip the side/base fabric to the stitching line, being careful not to clip through the stitching.
- Pivot, meet the edge of the side/base strip to the bottom edge of the front, using the clip to form a sharp corner.

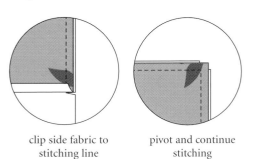

clip side fabric to stitching line

pivot and continue stitching

- Stitch along the bottom edge. Stop at the second corner. Clip, pivot, and complete the stitching. *Note: The strip may extend above the front at this time. Any excess will be trimmed evenly after the bag is assembled.*
- Attach the strip to the bag back in the same manner.

4. Finish the bag.
- Scallop all the seamed edges, being careful not to cut through the stitching.
- Scallop the top edges, trimming any excess side/base fabric even with the front and back.

- If the bag has the optional closure, fold the top of the bag toward the front 1". Fold again, meeting the back Velcro tape to the front Velcro tape.

fold

1"

If you prefer, you can enclose the seams on the lunch bag rather than having them exposed and scalloping the edges. Simply meet the *right* sides of the fabrics when you stitch the side/base to the front and back. Then turn the bag right side out and enjoy!

Nancy

CHAPTER 4

Sewing for the Bedroom & Den

Quilt-As-You-Go Reversible Quilt

There are two sides to every story, and the Reversible Quilt tells them both. The top of this quilt features a classic 18-patch pattern. Piecing and quilting time fly by because you build the quilt one panel at a time, quilting each panel as you go.

All of the prints featured on the top of the pictured quilt highlight birds and feather motifs, while the reverse side provides a great way of showcasing a favorite print fabric to give the bedroom a second color scheme.

Even rather detailed projects such as this quilt are attainable when they're divided into shorter, manageable increments of time. If you sew in 10, 20, 30, or 45 minute blocks of time, this quilt can become the showcase of your bedroom decor.

So whether you're feeling blue, or seeing red, the Reversible Quilt has you covered!

FINISHED SIZE

Approximately 75½" x 111"

MATERIALS NEEDED

Note: The following yardages of 44"/45" fabrics will make a twin size quilt. Adjust yardages for other quilt sizes.

Side A
- Fabric A: (blue feather) 1⅝ yd.
- Fabric B: (red print) 1½ yd.
- Fabric C: (vine grid) 4⅛ yd.
- Fabric D: (tan feather) ⅜ yd.
- Fabric E: (tan nest) ⅝ yd.

Side B
- Fabric F: (light blue print) 2⅞ yd.
- Fabric G: (dark blue print) 1¼ yd.
- Fabric H: (blue nest) 2¼ yd.
- Batting: 3¼ yd., 90" wide

Reverse side of quilt.

Making the Quilt

Note: All fabric cuts are 44"/45" crosswise strips unless otherwise indicated. All seam allowances are ¼" unless otherwise indicated.

1. Cut out the fabrics.
   Fabric A:
   - Cut three 3½" strips (side A corner blocks).
   - Cut seven 6" strips (side A inner borders).
   Fabric B:
   - Cut eight 3½" strips (side A sashing).
   - Cut two 9½" strips (side A sashing).
   Fabric C:
   - Cut three 9½" strips (side A center blocks).
   - Cut eight 12" strips (side A outer borders).
   - Cut eight 2½" strips (binding).
   Fabric D:
   - Cut one 9½" strip (side A center blocks).
   Fabric E:
   - Cut two 9½" strips (side A center blocks).
   Fabric F:
   - Cut eight 12" strips (side B outer borders).
   Fabric G:
   - Cut seven 6" strips (side B inner borders).
   Fabric H:
   - Cut one panel, the length of the main panel, approximately 75½" (side B).

2. Create the main panel stratas for side A. For each strata, join the lengthwise edges of the indicated strips, right sides together, in the order listed. (The following instructions will create a twin size quilt. Increase the number of sections prepared from each strata for other sizes.)
   - Strata 1:
     - Join a 3½" Fabric A, 9½" Fabric B, and 3½" Fabric A, right sides together.
     - Press the seams toward Fabric B.
     - Subcut the strata into seven 3½" sections.

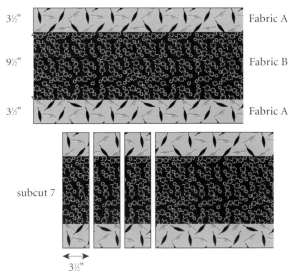

3½" Fabric A
9½" Fabric B
3½" Fabric A

subcut 7

3½"

- Strata 2:
  - Join a 3½" Fabric B, 9½" Fabric E, and 3½" Fabric B, right sides together.
  - Press the seams away from Fabric E.
  - Subcut into three 9½" sections.

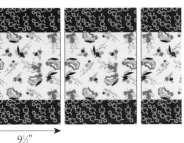

Fabric B

subcut 3 Fabric E

Fabric B

9½"

- Strata 3:
  - Join a 3½" Fabric B, 9½" Fabric C, and 3½" Fabric B, right sides together.
  - Press the seams away from Fabric C.
  - Subcut into three 9½" sections.

Fabric B

subcut 3 Fabric C

Fabric B

9½"

- Join the 9½" edges of the sections to form the panel, arranging them as shown. (Strata 1, 2, 1, 3, 1, 2, 1, 3, 1, 2, 1, 3, and 1.)

3. Create the add-on panel stratas for side A.
   - Strata 4:
     - Join a 9½" Fabric B and 3½" Fabric A.
     - Press the seam toward Fabric B.
     - Subcut into 12 3½" sections. Cut two additional sections from Strata 1. Remove one of the Fabric A strips.

Fabric B

Fabric A

3½" subcut 14

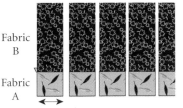

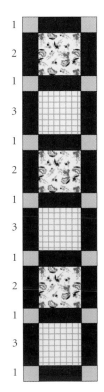

- **Strata 5:**
  - Join a 9½" Fabric C and 3½" Fabric B. Repeat, using 22" strips of each fabric to form a half strata. **20**
  - Press the seams toward Fabric B.
  - Subcut into six 9½" sections.

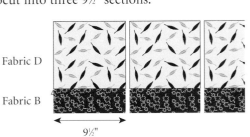

Fabric C

subcut 6

Fabric B

9½"

- **Strata 6:**
  - Join a 9½" Fabric D and 3½" Fabric B. **10**
  - Press the seam toward Fabric B.
  - Subcut into three 9½" sections.

Fabric D

subcut 3

Fabric B

9½"

- **Strata 7:**
  - Join a 9½" Fabric E and 3½" Fabric B. **10**
  - Press the seam toward Fabric B.
  - Subcut into three 9½" sections.

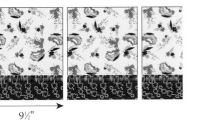

Fabric E

subcut 3

Fabric B

9½"

- Join the 9½" edges of the sections to form the first add-on panel, arranging them as shown. (Strata 4, 5, 4, 6, 4, 5, 4, 6, 4, 5, 4, 6, and 4.) **20**
- Join the 9½" edges of the sections to form the second add-on panel, arranging them as shown. (Strata 4, 7, 4, 5, 4, 7, 4, 5, 4, 7, 4, 5, and 4.) **20**

$\mathcal{S}$ave the remaining strata sections for other projects. For example, make throw pillows, or make a coordinating valance. (See page 71.) *Nancy*

first add-on panel   second add-on panel

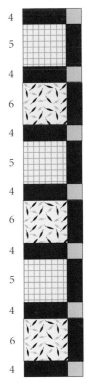
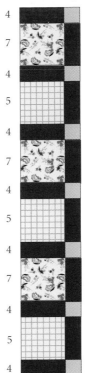

4. Cut the batting and backing strips. **20**
   - Choose an all-over print for the backing.
   - Backing: From Fabric H, subcut three panels the same sizes as the three Side A panels.
   - Batting: Cut three panels the same sizes as the three Side A panels.

5. Layer and machine quilt the main panel. **45**
   - Sandwich the batting between the wrong sides of the top panel and the backing.
   - Pin the sections together periodically to hold the layers together.
   - Zigzag around the cut edges with a medium width zigzag stitch.

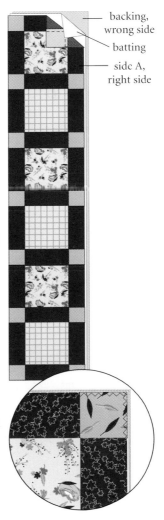

backing, wrong side
batting
side A, right side

- Machine quilt the main panel using one or more of these options.
  - Stitch in the ditch following the seam lines. Use the Edge-joining Foot, positioning the metal guide along the well of the seam.

Edge-joining Foot

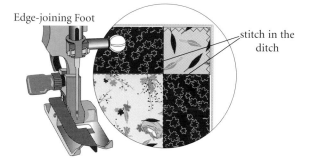

stitch in the ditch

  - Channel quilt, following an existing grid. Or mark and stitch lines about 2½" apart on the fabric.

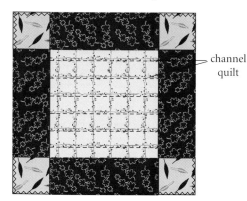

channel quilt

  - Enlarge and trace one of the motifs in the fabric print onto a water-soluble paper stabilizer such as WashAway™ Foundation Paper. Use that design as a quilting pattern. After stitching is completed, tear away the excess paper and remove any residue by spritzing it with water.

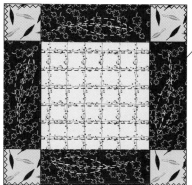

trace/stitch fabric motif

- Use free-motion stitching. Check your owner's manual for specific setup instructions for your machine. The following are general guidelines:
  - Lower the feed dogs.
  - Reduce the needle tension by two numbers or notches.

- Insert a Metafil or Metallica needle. These needles feature a fine shaft and a sharp point to virtually eliminate thread breakage, a specialized scarf to prevent skipped stitches, and an elongated eye to prevent thread stripping.
- Thread the needle with monofilament thread such as Madeira Monofil Thread, or match the thread to the fabric.
- Match the bobbin thread to the background fabric.
- Adjust the machine for a straight stitch.
- Attach a darning foot or a specialty foot such as the Big Foot®. The Big Foot provides just the right amount of pressure on the fabric, and the clear plastic foot affords excellent visibility. Both of these feet ride just above the surface of the fabric, allowing free movement, yet they prevent the fabric from bouncing back and forth.

Big Foot

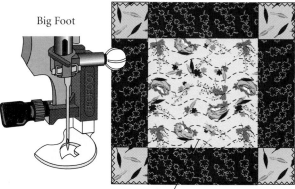

free-motion stitching

- Guide the movement of the fabric under the presser foot.

Stitch fast, but move the fabric slowly. The faster you stitch, the more even your stitching will be. Adjust your chair and machine position for greatest comfort to avoid getting a stiff neck as you stitch. And remember to breathe! Take slow, deep breaths, and enjoy the process.

Nancy

6. Attach the add-on panels.
   - Attach the first add-on panel to the main panel.

45

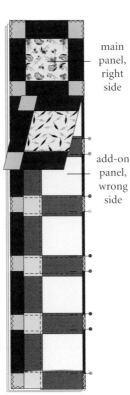

main panel, right side

add-on panel, wrong side

- Stack the add-on panel over the main panel, right sides together, meeting the panel ends and side edges. Pin at the seam intersections.
- Stack the backing panel to the underside of the main panel, right sides together. Pin.
- Stack and pin the batting on top of the backing panel.

batting

backing wrong side

- Stitch the add-on panel to the main panel using a ¼" seam.

fold out panel; zigzag edges together

- Fold out the add-on panel so the right sides are visible, enclosing the seam and meeting the cut edges. Pin, then zigzag the cut edges together.

• Machine quilt the add-on panel, using one or more of the techniques detailed on page 58.

I really like this technique because the bulk of the fabric is always to the left of the needle as you quilt. You never have to struggle with a large, heavy mass to the right of your needle!

Nancy

• Attach the second add-on panel, following the same technique.

45

attach second panel

7. Add the inner borders.

45

• Measure the length of the quilt. (It will be approximately 75½".) Piece 6" strips of Fabric A to make two side borders that equal that length.

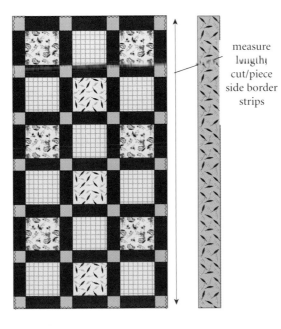

measure length; cut/piece side border strips

• Cut the batting and batting sections the same size as the side borders.

- Attach the side borders to the quilt, following the same technique as detailed for the add-on panels.

- Machine quilt the side borders.
- Measure the width of the quilt. (It will be approximately 51½".) Piece 6" strips of Fabric A to make top and bottom borders that length.

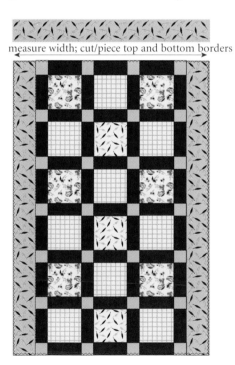

measure width; cut/piece top and bottom borders

- Attach the top and bottom borders, following the same technique as for the side borders.

8. Add outer borders, using the same technique as for the inner borders.

45

9. Bind the quilt using a double fold French binding.

- Join 2½" crosswise strips, right sides together, using a diagonal seam to reduce the bulk. Join enough strips to equal the outer measurement of the quilt plus 6" to 8". Trim the seam and press it open.

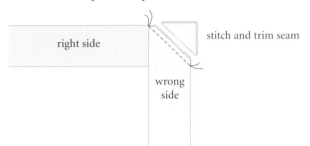

right side

stitch and trim seam

wrong side

- Cut one end of the strip at a 45° angle; fold in ¼".

fold in ¼"

wrong side

- Press a ¼" strip of paper-backed fusible web to the folded-under edge of the binding. Fold the binding in half lengthwise, wrong sides together. Press.

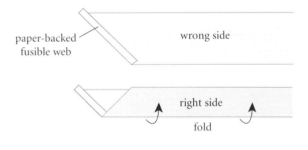

paper-backed fusible web

wrong side

right side

fold

- Mark the right side of the quilt ¼" from each corner.

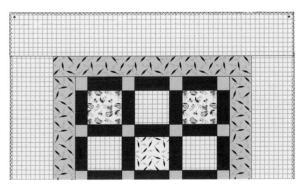

- Meet the angle-cut end of the binding (the end with the paper-backed fusible web) to the right side of the quilt top, meeting the raw edges and starting in the center of one side. Stitch the binding to the quilt with a scant ¼" seam, beginning 4" from the end of the binding and stopping at the marked point at the first corner. Lock the stitches.

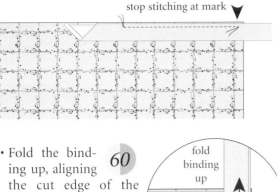

stop stitching at mark

- Fold the binding up, aligning the cut edge of the binding with the cut edge of the quilt.
- Fold the binding down, meeting the binding fold to the top edge of the quilt and the binding cut edge to the side edges. Stitch a ¼" seam on the side, starting at the folded edge.
- Repeat at the remaining corners.
- Join the binding ends as detailed for bias tape, pages 95-96. Stitch the remainder of the seam.

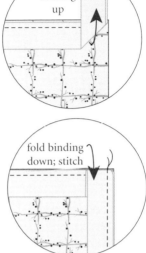

fold binding up

fold binding down; stitch

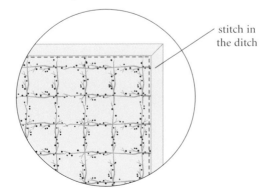

insert binding end; stitch

- Fold and press the binding away from the quilt. Then fold the binding to the wrong side, covering the stitching line and tucking in the corners to form miters.
- Pin the binding in place. Secure the remaining edge of the binding by stitching in the ditch from the right side, sewing in the well of the seam through all the layers to catch the folded edge on the back of the quilt.

stitch in the ditch

Complete your bed ensemble with an attractive Pillow Sham designed to coordinate with the Reversible Quilt. Your bed ensemble will clearly be a candidate for the best dressed category.

FINISHED SIZE

Approximately 24½" x 33"

MATERIALS NEEDED

(44"/45" wide fabrics)

	One Sham	Two Shams
• Fabric A	½ yd.	⅞ yd.
• Fabric B	¼ yd.	½ yd.
• Fabric C	⅜ yd.	⅜ yd.
• Fabric D	⅛ yd.	⅛ yd.
• Fabric E	¾ yd.	1½ yd.
• Muslin	¾ yd.	1½ yd.
• Batting	¾ yd.	1½ yd.
• ¾" to 1" buttons	6	12

Pillow Sham

Making the Pillow Sham

(Makes one sham)

Note: *All seam allowances are ¼" unless otherwise noted.*

1. Cut the fabrics.
   - Fabric A: Cut two crosswise strips 3½" x 24½" (left and right outer borders).
     Cut two crosswise strips 3½" x 27" (top and bottom outer borders).
   - Fabric B: Cut two crosswise strips 3½" wide. Subcut each into a 3½" x 21½" strip (top/bottom inner border) and a 3½" x 13" strip (left/right inner border).

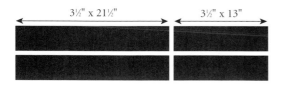

3½" x 21½"   3½" x 13"

   - Fabric C: Cut one 13" x 21½" rectangle (center).
   - Fabric D: Cut four 3½" squares (corner squares).

We centered and "fussy cut" bird motifs from a fabric print for the corner squares on our sham. Doing that may require additional fabric to get the designs positioned precisely where you want them. You'll want to take that into account when you purchase fabric and cut out the squares. *Nancy*

   - Fabric E: Cut one crosswise 25" strip. Subcut as follows:
     - Cut one 15" x 25" rectangle (top button flap).
     - Cut one 25" x 28" rectangle (lower back).
   - Muslin: Cut one 24½" x 27" rectangle.
   - Batting: Cut one 24½" x 27" rectangle.

2. Add the inner borders to the front of the Pillow Sham. *20*

- Meet the Fabric B top and bottom inner borders to the lengthwise edges of the Fabric C center, with right sides together. Stitch the seams and press them toward the borders.

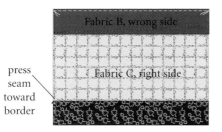

press seam toward border

- Piece and add the side borders.
  - Meet the 3½" Fabric D corner squares to the short ends of the Fabric B left and right inner borders, with right sides together. Press the seams toward the borders.

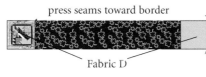

press seams toward border

Fabric D

  - Meet the left and right inner borders to the short edges of the Fabric C center, with right sides together. Stitch the seams and press them toward the borders.

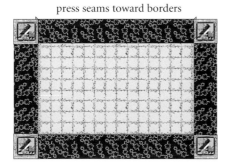

press seams toward borders

- Add the outer borders.
  - Meet the top and bottom Fabric A outer borders to the sham, with right sides together. Stitch the seams and press them toward the outer borders.

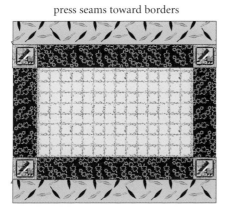

press seams toward borders

  - Add the left and right Fabric A outer borders to the sham using the same technique.

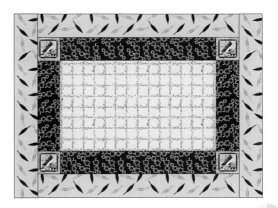

3. Layer and quilt the top of the sham. **20**
   - Layer the sham in this order: muslin, batting, sham, right side up.
   - Pin the layers together. Zigzag around the outer edges.

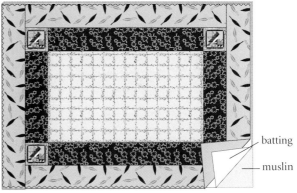

batting

muslin

zigzag edges

   - Machine quilt using one or more of the techniques detailed for the Quilt As You Go Reversible Quilt, page 58.

4. Prepare the back of the Pillow Sham. **30**
   - Prepare the top button flap.
     - Fold under and press a double 2" hem along one 25" edge of the Fabric E flap.

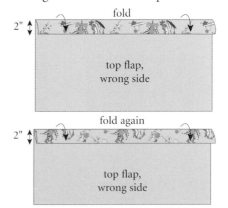

fold

2"

top flap, wrong side

fold again

2"

top flap, wrong side

   - Topstitch the hem in place.

topstitch hem

top flap, wrong side

- Measure and mark the positions for the button-holes on the hem. We placed two buttonholes 1½" apart at the center of the flap, then positioned additional sets of buttonholes 6" from the short edges, spacing them 1½" apart.
- Stitch vertical buttonholes sized to fit the buttons at each marked position, adding a stabilizer under the buttonhole for added reinforcement.
- Cut open the buttonholes.

• Prepare the lower back section.
  - Fold under and press a double 2" hem along one 25" edge of the Fabric E lower back.
  - Topstitch the hem in place.

stitch 2" double hem

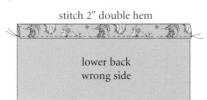

lower back
wrong side

• Overlap the top button flap onto the lower back section so the size corresponds to the front of the Pillow Sham. Machine baste the overlapped edges.

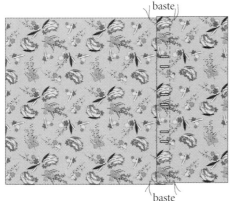

• Mark the button positions on the lower back panel to correspond to the buttonhole positions on the button flap.
• Stitch the buttons in place.

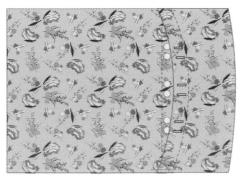

5. Join the sham sections.
  • Pin the front and back together, right sides together, meeting the cut edges. Stitch ¼" seams around all four sides of the Pillow Sham, wrapping the corners.
    - Stitch one lengthwise seam, stitching from edge to edge. Press the seam.

stitch first edge

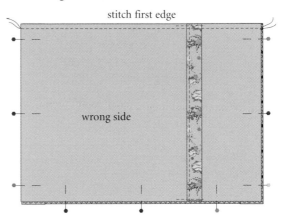

wrong side

- Fold the seam along the stitching line. The seam allowance will fold, or "wrap" toward the inside of the sham.
- Stitch the adjacent seam, beginning at the wrapped corner and stitching to the next edge. Press.
- Repeat until all four edges have been stitched.

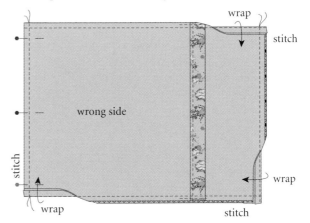

wrong side

• Turn the sham right side out. Press.
• Stitch in the ditch around the inner edge of the outer border to create a flange on the Pillow Sham.

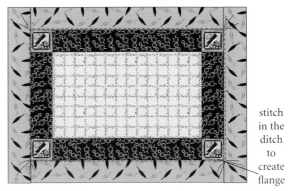

stitch in the ditch to create flange

• Insert the pillow through the flap opening; button the flap to secure the pillow.

Made-to-Order Pillowcases

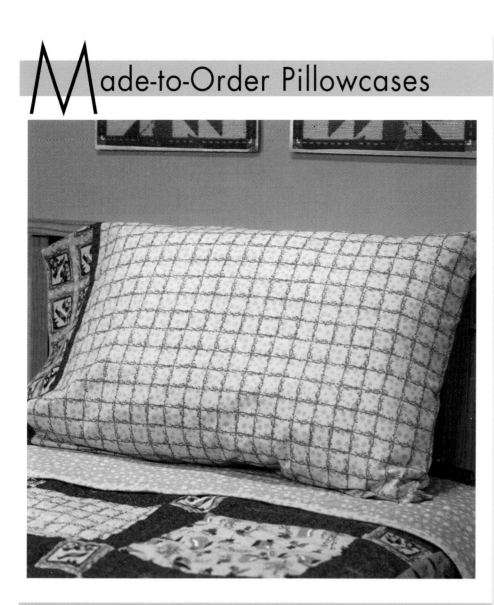

Make pillowcases to coordinate with any season, holiday, or décor, or to fit any size pillows, with these Made-to-Order Pillowcases. Start with a pillowcase fabric, then blend it with a border fabric and a contrasting or coordinating piping. The result: your pillows will be as well-dressed as the rest of your décor.

These pillowcases are a great beginning project for a new sewer, too. The sewing is "sew" easy. Get creative with your favorite fabrics and trims and individualize the cases to suit your personality and décor.

FINISHED SIZE

Approximately 20¼" x 31¾"

MATERIALS NEEDED

(44"/45" fabrics)
- Fabric A: 1⅜ yd.
- Fabric B: ⅛ yd.
- Fabric C: ⅝ yd.

Making the Pillowcases

(Makes two pillowcases)

Note: All seam allowances are ¼" unless otherwise indicated.

1. Cut out the pillowcase sections. **10**
   - Fabric A: Cut two 28" x 41" rectangles (pillowcases).
   - Fabric B: Cut two 2" x 41" strips (piping).
   - Fabric C: Cut two 9" x 41" rectangles (borders).

2. Sew the main section of each pillowcase. **10**
   - Fold the Fabric A rectangle, right sides together, meeting the 28" edges. Stitch the side seam.
   - Press the seam flat; zigzag or serge the edges together.

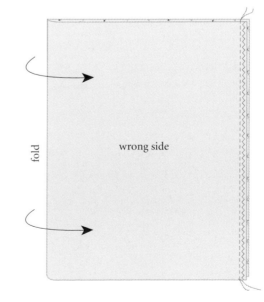

fold

wrong side

- Fold the seam along the stitching line, wrapping it toward the center of the pillowcase. Begin stitching at the fold and sew one end of the pillowcase closed. This is a "wrapped corner."

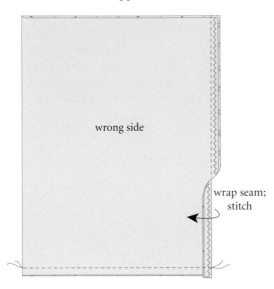

wrong side

wrap seam; stitch

- Press the seam flat; zigzag or serge the edges together.
- Turn the case right side out.

3. Add the border and piping strips to each pillowcase. **30**
   - Seam each Fabric C border and Fabric B piping strip, right sides together, meeting the short edges to form circles. Press the seams open.

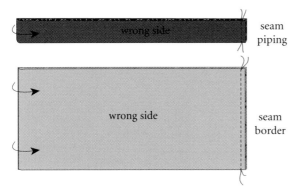

wrong side — seam piping

wrong side — seam border

- Press the border and piping bands in half, wrong sides together, meeting the cut edges.

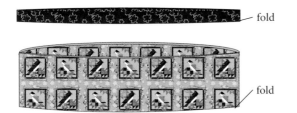

fold

fold

- Machine baste the piping to the border, meeting the cut edges and matching the seamlines.

baste piping to border

- Slip the border over the pillowcase, with the piping next to the right side of the pillowcase, matching the seamlines. Stitch the seam.

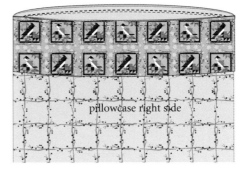

pillowcase right side

- Serge or zigzag the raw edges. Press the seam toward the pillowcase.
- *Optional:* Topstitch along the edge of Fabric A to secure the seam.

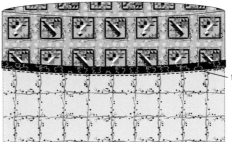

topstitch

These pillowcases make great gifts, too! Select a novelty fabric print with pizzazz and create pillowcases to go. Match the fabric to a seasonal holiday, or select a fabric that depicts the interests or personality of the recipient. It's a quick and easy way to personalize a gift.

Nancy

Duvet Cover

Give your comforter new life with an attractive Duvet Cover. The cover slips over the comforter like a giant pillow-case. The sewing is easy, and with two coordinating fabrics and a little sewing time, your comforter can have a fresh start.

Materials Needed

(The following yardages and instructions are for 44"/45" fabric and cover a twin-size comforter. Additional yardage is required for making full and queen sizes.)

- Fabric A: 6 yd.
- Fabric B: 4⅝ yd.
- Nine to 11 buttons, ¾" to 1" in diameter
- 6 yd. ribbon, ¼" to ½" wide

Making the Duvet Cover

Note: Use ¼" seam allowances unless otherwise indicated.

1. Measure the comforter. The Duvet Cover **5** should fit snugly around the comforter, giving the comforter a little "pouf." Standard sizes are as follows, but measure to be sure.
   - Twin: 70" x 90"
   - Double: 85" x 95"
   - Queen: 90" x 95"

   measure comforter

2. Cut the fabrics. **10**
   - Fabric A: Using the full fabric width, cut two 90" long panels (backing). Using the full fabric width, cut two 18" panels (button flap).
   - Fabric B: Using the full fabric width, cut two 82" panels (lower front panel).

3. Join the Duvet **15** sections.
   - Subcut and rejoin the fabric sections.
     - Cut one 90" Fabric A panel in half lengthwise, making two 90" half panels.

½ panel   ½ panel

90"

cut one panel in half

- Sew one half panel to each lengthwise side of the full panel, right sides together. This centers the design.

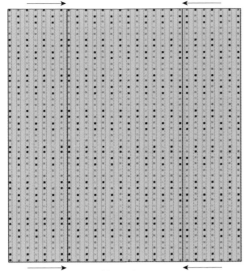

join half panels to center

- Repeat for both the 82" Fabric B panels and the 18" button flap panels.
• Trim each seamed panel to 70" wide, centering the middle panel so equal amounts are cut from each edge.

trim panel to 70"

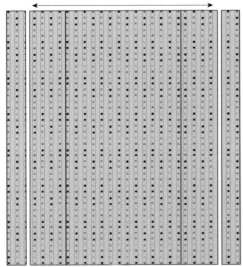

Although you might think you need to make the fabric panels wider than the comforter measurement to allow for seam allowances, I prefer cutting the panels the same size as the comforter. That makes the comforter fit snugly inside the Duvet Cover and adds an attractive "pouf." *Nancy*

4. Create the top button flap. **20**
  • Fold under and press a double 2" hem along one lengthwise edge of the flap.

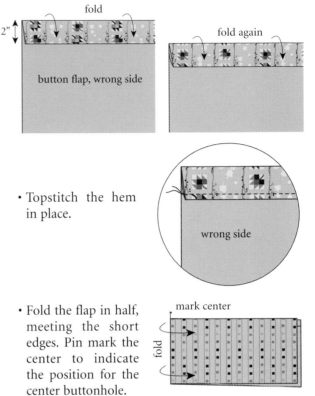

  • Topstitch the hem in place.

  • Fold the flap in half, meeting the short edges. Pin mark the center to indicate the position for the center buttonhole.
  • Measure and mark positions for additional buttonholes, spacing them 6" to 7" apart.

mark buttonhole placements

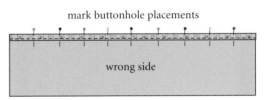

wrong side

  • Stitch vertical buttonholes sized to fit the buttons at each pin mark, adding a stabilizer under the buttonhole for added reinforcement.
  • Cut open the buttonholes.

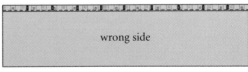

wrong side

5. Prepare the lower front section of the Duvet Cover. **10**
  • Fold under and press a double 2" hem along one 70" edge.
  • Topstitch the hem in place.

fold and press 2" double hem; topstitch

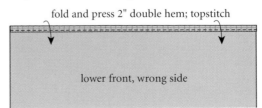

lower front, wrong side

6. Join the Duvet Cover sections.

- Overlap the top button flap onto the lower front panel. The combined length of the two panels must equal 90" (or the length of the comforter).

overlap to equal comforter length

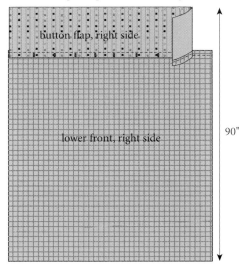

button flap, right side

lower front, right side

90"

- Machine baste the overlapped side edges of the panels.
- Mark the button positions on the lower front panel to correspond to the buttonhole positions on the button flap.
- Stitch the buttons in place.

stitch buttons

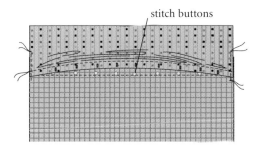

- Pin the front and back layers together, right sides together, meeting the cut edges.

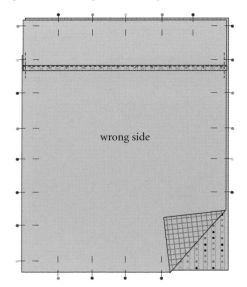

wrong side

- Add the ribbon ties.
  - Cut 14 pieces of ribbon, 6" to 7" long.
  - Position and pin a tie 1" from each corner, aligning one end of the tie with the cut edge of the back side of the Duvet Cover.
  - Pin the remaining ties evenly spaced around the exterior of the Duvet Cover.

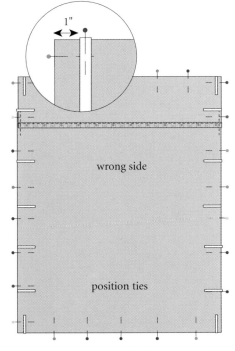

1"

wrong side

position ties

- Stitch ¼" seams around all four sides of the cover, wrapping the corners as follows.
  - Stitch one lengthwise seam, stitching from edge to edge. Press the seam flat.

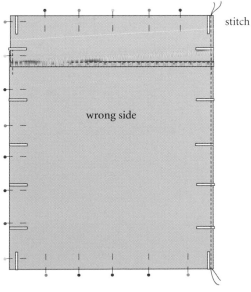

stitch

wrong side

- Fold the seam along the first stitching line. The seam allowance should fold, or "wrap" toward the inside of the panel.
- Stitch the adjacent seam, beginning at the wrapped corner and stitching to the next edge. Press the seam.

- Fold the seam along the stitching line; continue stitching.

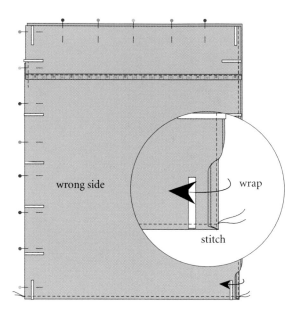

wrong side

wrap

stitch

- Repeat until all four edges have been stitched.

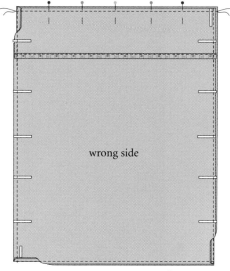

wrong side

wrap next corner; stitch

7. Cut and attach 14 similar ties to the corresponding positions on the comforter.

10

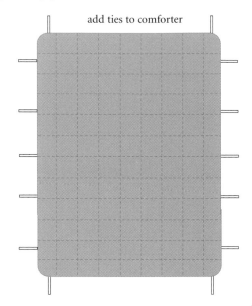

add ties to comforter

8. Tie the comforter to the Duvet Cover, meeting the comforter to the wrong side of the back of the cover.

5

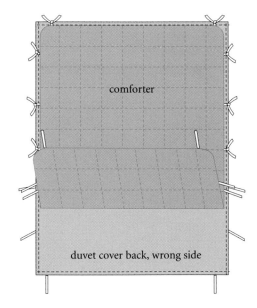

comforter

duvet cover back, wrong side

9. Turn the Duvet Cover right side out and slip the comforter inside through the opening on the flap.

5

Versatile Valances

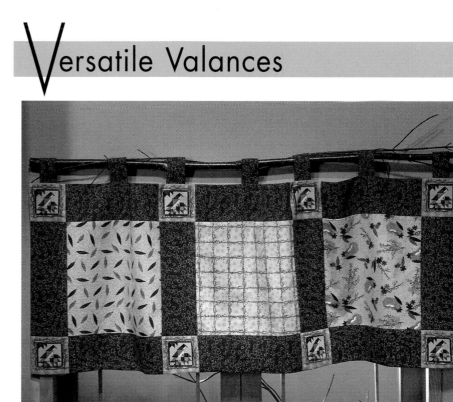

Making the Valance

The old adage says, "Waste not, want not." Rather than shelving some of the remnants from the Reversible Quilt, use several of the extra fabric strata segments to add yet another coordinating element to your decorating scheme. Simplicity is the key with this versatile window treatment. Three blocks, borders, a backing, and some tabs are all you need.

FINISHED SIZE
Approximately 15" x 38½"

MATERIALS NEEDED
(44"/45" fabrics)
- Fabric A: ⅛ yd. (If cutting specific designs in the blocks, be sure the design is centered within the block. Adjust fabric yardage accordingly.)
- Fabric B: ¾ yd.
- One Strata 3 block (see Reversible Quilt, page 56).
- One Strata 6 block (see Reversible Quilt, page 57).
- One Strata 7 block (see Reversible Quilt, page 57).

Note: *All seam allowances are ¼" unless otherwise noted.*

1. Cut out the fabrics. **15**
   - Fabric A: Cut eight 3½" squares (border blocks).
   - Fabric B: Cut six 3½" x 9½" rectangles (borders).
     Cut one crosswise 3" strip (tabs).
     Cut one 15½" x 39" rectangle (backing).
   - Strata 3: Cut one 9½" block.
   - Strata 6: Cut one 9½" block.
   - Strata 7: Cut one 9½" block.

2. Prepare the top and bottom border strips. **10**
   - Join the 3½" Fabric A border blocks to the Fabric B borders with ¼" seams, right sides together, in this order: Fabric A, Fabric B, Fabric A, Fabric B, Fabric A, Fabric B, Fabric A. Press all seams in one direction.

press all seams in one direction

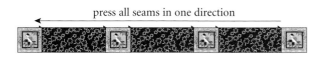

- Make a second border strip using the same sequence.

As an alternative to having specific motifs in each of the border blocks, you could cut 3½" sections from Stratas 1 and 4 from the Reversible Quilt (see page 56) and seam them to make the top and bottom borders.

Nancy

3. Join the center section of the valance. ⑩

- Rotate the Strata 7 block so the 3½" border strip is at the left.
- Join the 9½" blocks, right sides together, in this order: Strata 7, Strata 3, Strata 6. Press the seams in the opposite direction of those for the border strips.

press →

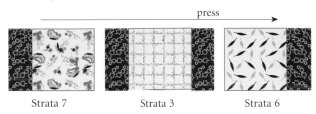

Strata 7   Strata 3   Strata 6

4. Join the top and bottom border strips to the center section, right sides together. Press the seams toward the borders. ⑩

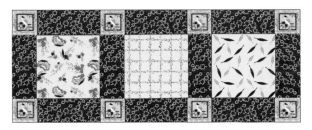

5. Prepare the tabs. ⑩

- Meet the lengthwise edges of the 3" Fabric B strip, right sides together. Stitch a ¼" seam.

meet right sides;
stitch

- Turn the strip right side out using a #5 Fasturn.
  - Place the stitched tube over the Fasturn cylinder. Finger press the seams open.
  - Wrap and fold one end of the tube tightly over the end of the cylinder. Insert the wire into the cylinder from the handle end. Turn the hook clockwise (to the right) so it goes through the fabric and catches it.

turn clockwise

- Gently pull the wire back through the cylinder, turning the tube right side out. To prevent undue strain on the turning wire, manually slide additional fabric up on the cylinder as some of the fabric is drawn through the cylinder. Do not turn the hook, or it may release from the fabric.
- When the turned tube reaches the opening at the end of the Fasturn handle, release the hook by turning it counterclockwise (to the left). Complete the turning by pulling the fabric, rather than the hook. Doing so prevents the wire from breaking.

pull through cylinder

turn counterclockwise

- Press the strip, centering the seam.

- Cut the strip into seven 5" sections.

6. Position the tabs on the valance. ⑤

- Fold each tab in half, meeting cut the edges. Press the folds.

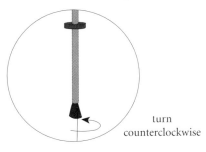

fold tab in half

• Place the tabs on the right side of the valance, meeting the cut edges. Each tab should be centered over one portion of the top border strip. Baste the tabs in place.

baste tabs in place

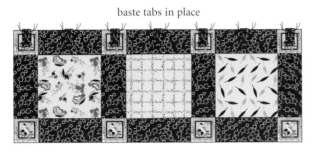

7. Join the front and back of the valance.

15

• Pin the front and back sections together, right sides together, meeting the cut edges. Stitch ¼" seams around all four sides of the valance, wrapping the corners.
  - Beginning with one of the side edges, stitch one side seam, sewing from edge to edge. Press the seam.

stitch one seam

backing wrong side

  - Fold the seam along the stitching line. The seam allowance will fold, or "wrap" toward the inside of the seam.

- Stitch the adjacent seam, beginning at the wrapped corner and stitching to the next edge. Press.

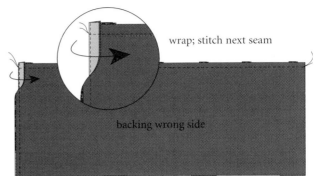

wrap; stitch next seam

backing wrong side

- Repeat until all four edges have been stitched, leaving a 6" opening at the center of the lower edge for turning.

backing wrong side

leave opening to turn

• Turn the valance right side out. Press.
• Hand stitch the opening closed.

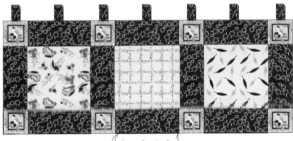

hand stitch

Traditionally, quilts are made with three layers: a backing, batting, and quilt top. Here's a two-layer quilt, where high-loft fleece serves as both the backing and the batting to create a comfy blanket. You'll be pleased at how this outerwear fabric doubles as a perfect quilting component.

FINISHED SIZE

Approximately 42" x 54"

MATERIALS NEEDED

- Fabric A: (high-loft fleece) 1⅓ yd.
- Fabric B: 1½ yd. (44"/45" wide)

Fleece/Fabric Throw

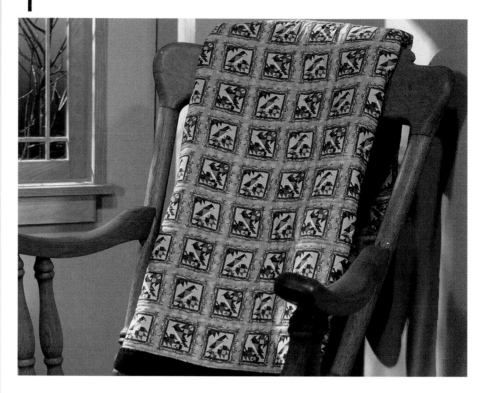

Making the Throw

1. Layer and mark the throw.

   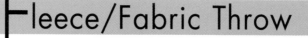

   - Cut fleece 3" to 4" longer and wider than Fabric B. This provides 1½" to 2" quilt borders around all sides of the quilt top. Adjust the borders to be as narrow or wide as you prefer, but keep them uniform on all four edges.
   - Center Fabric B on the fleece, wrong sides together, measuring to ensure that the borders are uniform on each side.
   - Using a chalk marker, mark a series of parallel quilting lines 3" apart for channel stitching.

Chaco-Liner is a no-mess way to mark. The lipstick-tube-shaped marker dispenses an accurate thin line of powder on any weight fabric. When marks are no longer needed, they can be easily brushed away. Or, as another option use a Chacopel pencil.

Nancy

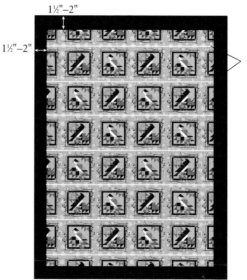

1½"–2"

1½"–2"

mark quilting lines

- Pin the two layers together, starting in the center and working to the outer edges. Curved basting pins will help you complete this step quickly. These pins are just the right angle for easy, comfortable insertion, and they can safely remain in the fabric until the project is complete.

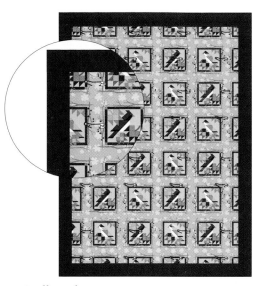

- Roll the sides of the throw to the middle and clamp with Jaws™. Jaws are flexible quilting notions that keep the quilt neatly rolled during machine quilting. Just open and twist the Jaws to position them on the rolled throw.

2. Set up the machine for machine quilting. **5**
   - Replace the conventional presser foot with a Walking Foot to help the layers feed evenly through the machine. (If your machine has dual feed, engage it and attach an Open Toe or Appliqué Foot.)
   - Use matching thread in the needle and the bobbin.
   - Adjust the machine for a slightly longer straight stitch, approximately eight to 10 stitches per inch, to allow for the bulk of the fabric layers.
   - If possible, adjust the machine to stop in "needle down" position.

3. Channel stitch the quilt, securing the threads at each end. **20**
   - Choose one marked line in the center of the quilt. Stitch along that line, beginning and ending the stitches at the Fabric B edges.

stitch down center

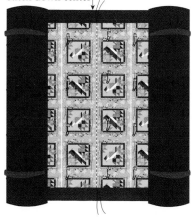

- Stitch additional lines, alternating the direction of the adjacent rows to prevent the fabric from shifting.

channel stitch; alternating direction

Jaws ___

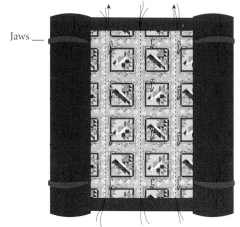

4. Finish the edges of the quilt. **20**
   - Miter the corners of the fleece.
     - Diagonally fold the fleece to the right side at each corner of the quilt top, folding at the corner of Fabric B. Trim the excess folded fleece ¼" from the corner.

fold in

trim

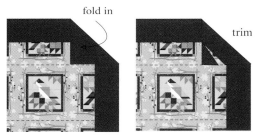

   - Fold the fleece borders to the right side, over the quilt top. Pin the borders in place, mitering the corners. Or for an even easier way to secure the fleece, use Binding and Hem Clips.
   - Stitch along the cut edges, sewing from the right side with a straight stitch or zigzag.

stitch along cut edges

   - Stitch the mitered corners to secure them.

secure mitered corners

CHAPTER 5

Sewing for the Baby's Room

Trip-Around-the-Nursery Baby Blanket

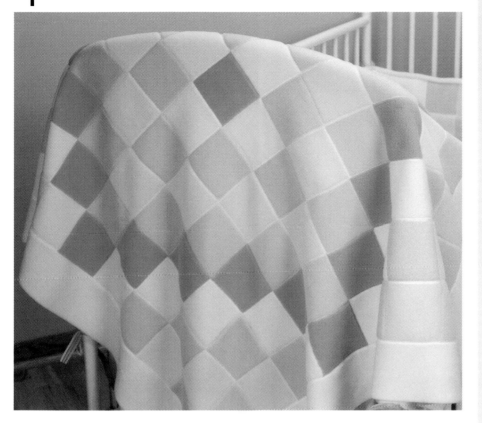

For years, quilters have stitched the popular "Trip Around the World" pattern. We adapted that pattern to make this high-loft fleece baby blanket. Because fleece fabrics like Polarfleece or Polartec don't ravel, you can use alternate seaming techniques. Instead of joining sections with conventional right sides together seams, use this butted and stitched edge-joined seam. The result: an attractive blanket sure to be the delight of any nursery.

FINISHED SIZE

Approximately 52" x 52"

MATERIALS NEEDED

- ¾ yd. white high-loft fleece
- ⅓ yd. pink high-loft fleece
- ⅓ yd. yellow high-loft fleece
- ⅓ yd. mint green high-loft fleece
- ⅓ yd. blue high-loft fleece

Making the Blanket

1. Cut the fabrics. **15**
   - White fleece: Cut four 4" crosswise strips (borders).
     Cut two 4" crosswise strips (strata).
   - Pink fleece: Cut two 4" crosswise strips (strata).
   - Yellow fleece: Cut two 4" crosswise strips (strata).
   - Mint green fleece: Cut two 4" crosswise strips (strata).
   - Blue fleece: Cut two 4" crosswise strips (strata).
     Cut one 4" square (center).

2. Prepare two of the following strata, joining the 4" strips with edge-joined seams. **30**
   - Arrange the strips in the following order: blue, mint green, yellow, pink, and white.

> Check that all strips are right side up. Remember, fleece curls to the wrong side when it is stretched on the crossgrain. *Nancy*

- Set up the sewing machine for edge-joined seaming.
  - Engage the dual feed if your machine has that feature.
  - Thread both the needle and the bobbin with all-purpose thread.

- Replace the conventional presser foot with an Edge-joining Foot. A guide in the center of the foot keeps fabric precisely aligned for even stitching.

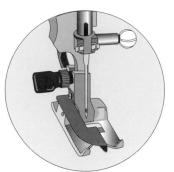

- Use a balanced tension.
- Set the machine for a feather stitch or a multi-zigzag with a length of 2.0 and a width of 6.0 or 7.0. Or use a wide zigzag and shorten the length to 1.0.
- Test the stitching with fabric scraps. Adjust the settings as needed.
• Join the strips in the strata.
- Butt the cut edges of the fleece strips to either side of the guide on the Edge-joining Foot to ensure that the stitching is centered as the two pieces arc seamed.

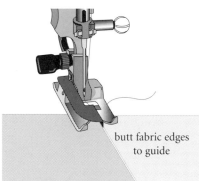

butt fabric edges to guide

- Seam the strips in the sequence shown, taking care to avoid stretching the fabric.

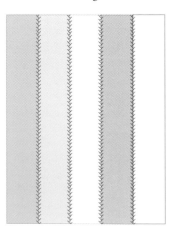

- Steam press the strata. **Important Note:** *Do not touch the surface of the iron to the fabric, as it*

could damage the surface of the fabric. Instead, hold the iron several inches above the fabric, steam the area, and finger press.

3. Cut the strata to prepare quilt sections.   **30**
   • Cut the stratas into 24 strips, 4" long.
   • Stack eight strips, positioning the blue fleece on top. Label the group "Section A."

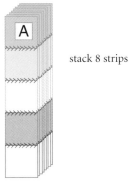

stack 8 strips

   • Stitch each of the remaining 16 sections into a tube, using an edge-joining seam.
   • Prepare four strips of each of the following quilt sections by removing the stitching between the indicated colors.

stitch tube

   - Section B: Remove the stitching between the blue and mint green squares. Stack the four strips with mint green on top and label them "Section B."
   - Section C: Remove the stitching between the mint green and yellow squares. Stack the four strips with yellow on top and label them "Section C."
   - Section D: Remove the stitching between the yellow and the pink squares. Stack the four strips with pink on top and label them "Section D."
   - Section E: Remove the stitching between the pink and the white squares. Stack the four strips with white on top and label them "Section E."

4. Join the quilt sections to form squares.   **30**
   • Place Sections A through E next to each other, starting with Section A at the left.

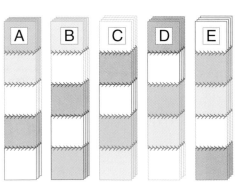

stack and label sections

- Join the Section A strips to Section B strips.
  - Meet one strip of each section, butting the edges and matching seam intersections. Tape-baste the sections together with small pieces of Sewer's Fix-it Tape. Use as little tape as possible to reduce the potential for pulling or distorting the fleece nap.

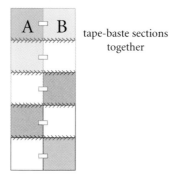

tape-baste sections together

- Join the two sections with a feather stitch. Do not raise the presser foot or cut threads.
- Butt the next pair of sections to the first pair; continue stitching.
- Repeat, chain stitching four sets of the pairs.
- Seal the thread ends of each pair with a tiny drop of Fray Check. Then cut the threads between each of the stitched pairs.

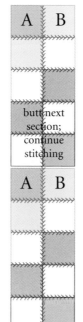

butt next section; continue stitching

cut threads between sections

- Repeat, joining the Section C strips to Section D strips, again stitching four sets of the pairs.

- Stitch pairs A/B to pairs C/D, following the same technique. Repeat, stitching four four-strip sections.

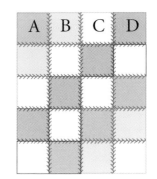

- Stitch a Section E strip to each of four-strip sections to form four squares.

5. Arrange and join the quilt sections.
   - Place the four squares on a flat surface with the blue fleece positioned in each of the four outer corners, allowing space between the squares.
   - Place a Section A strip between each square, with the blue fleece along the outer edge of the design.

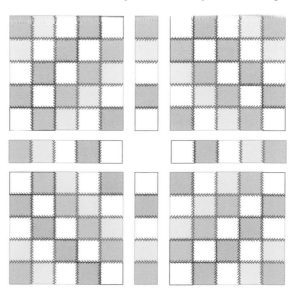

- Place the 4" blue fleece square in the center of the design.

- Stitch all the sections together using edge-joining seams.
  - Join the upper left and right squares to the center strip.

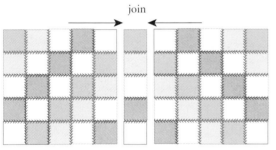

  - Join the left and right middle strips to the blue center square.

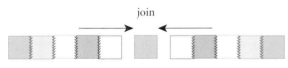

  - Join the lower left and right squares to the center strip.

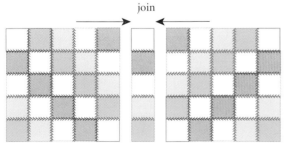

  - Join the upper section to the middle strip.
  - Join the lower section to the middle strip.

6. Add the borders.
   - Cut two 44" lengths and two 52" lengths from the border strips.
   - Place the quilt on a flat surface and position the 44" borders on the left and right edges of the quilt.
   - Pin the border to the quilt at the seam intersections. Stitch the border using edge-joined seams.

- Repeat, adding the 52" borders to the top and bottom edges.

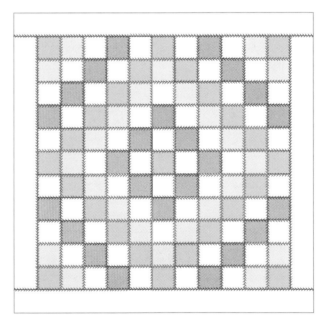

7. *Optional:* Finish the outer edges of the quilt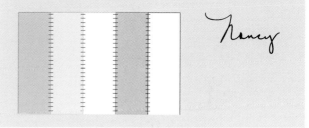
in one of these ways.
- Stitch around the outer edge with a feather stitch.
- Turn under the edge ½" and stitch with a feather stitch or a multizigzag.
- Bind the edges with a satin binding as indicated on pages 86-87.

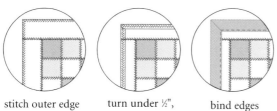

stitch outer edge   turn under ½",   bind edges
                     stitch outer edge

As an option to using edge-joined seams for making this quilt, you could use serged flatlocked seams. If you've never used a flatlock stitch before, this is the perfect time to start, since fleece is a very forgiving fabric. Thread the serger with all-purpose serger thread. Then do some test stitching using fabric scraps. If the seam buckles, try lengthening the stitch and loosening the needle tensions. Check your serger owner's manual for specific recommendations for your machine.

Nancy

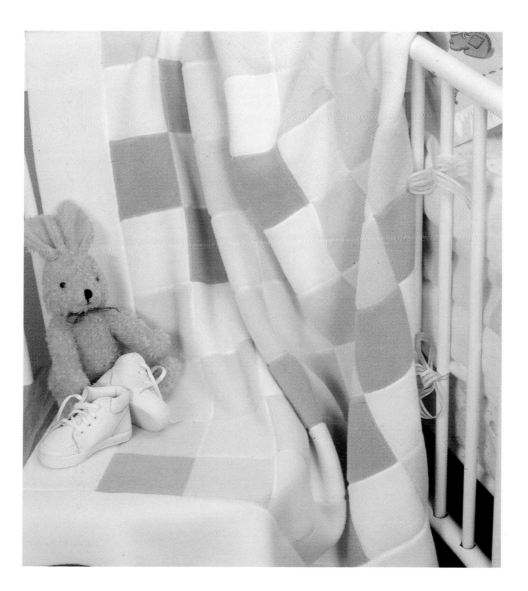

Baby will rest in cozy comfort with these bumper pads, made with the same seaming technique as the Trip-Around-the-Nursery Baby Blanket, lining the crib. Two layers of high-loft batting are sandwiched between two layers of fleece, transforming the crib into a secure and cushioned environment. Use the same five colors of fleece selected for the blanket to dress the nursery in style.

FINISHED SIZE

Approximately 12" x 168"

MATERIALS NEEDED

- 1½ yd. white high-loft fleece
- ¾ yd. mint green high-loft fleece
- ¾ yd. yellow high-loft fleece
- ⅛ yd. blue high-loft fleece
- ⅛ yd. pink high-loft fleece
- ½ yd. 100" wide high-loft batting
- 8 yd. grosgrain ribbon, ⅜" to ½" wide

Cozy Crib Bumper Pads

Making the Bumper Pads

1. Cut out the fabrics. **20**
   - White fleece: Cut eight crosswise strips, 4" wide.
     Cut six crosswise strips, 2" wide (binding).
   - Mint green fleece: Cut five crosswise strips, 4" wide.
   - Yellow fleece: Cut five crosswise strips, 4" wide.
   - Blue fleece: Cut one crosswise strip, 4" wide.
   - Pink fleece: Cut one crosswise strip, 4" wide.
   - Ribbon: Cut 12 ties, 24" long.

2. Set up the sewing machine for edge-joined seaming. **5**
   - Engage the dual feed if your machine has that feature.
   - Thread both the needle and the bobbin with all-purpose thread.
   - Replace the conventional pressing foot with an Edge-joining Foot. A guide in the center of the foot keeps the fabric precisely aligned for even stitching.
   - Use a balanced tension.

- Set the machine for a feather stitch or a multizigzag with a length of 2.0 and a width of 6.0 or 7.0. Or use a wide zigzag and shorten the length to 1.0.
- Test the stitching with fabric scraps. Adjust the settings as needed.

3. Prepare three strata sets, joining the 4" strips with edge-joined seams. **30**
   - Arrange the strips in the following order:
     - Strata A: (make two) mint green, yellow, mint green.

Strata A

- Strata B: (make one) yellow, mint green, yellow.

Strata B

- Strata C: (make four) blue, yellow, mint green, pink.

Strata C

Check that all strips are right side up. Remember, fleece curls to the wrong side when it is stretched on the crossgrain. *Nancy*

• Join the strips in each strata.
  - Butt the cut edges of the fleece strips to either side of the guide on the Edge-joining Foot to ensure that the stitching is centered as the two pieces are seamed.
  - Seam the strips in the sequences listed, taking care to avoid stretching the fabric.
  - Steam press the strata.

Don't touch the surface of the iron to the fabric as you press, as it could damage the fabric. Instead, hold the iron several inches above the fabric, steam the area, and finger press. *Nancy*

4. Cut the strata into 4" segments as follows: **20**
  • Strata A: Cut 24 segments.
  • Strata B: Cut 12 segments.

• Strata C: Cut 12 segments.

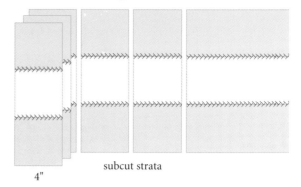

subcut strata

4"

5. Join the segments to form blocks. **30**
  • Create 12 nine-patch blocks.
    - Butt the Strata A segments along the top and bottom edges of each Strata B segment, matching the seams.
    - Feather stitch along the 12" edges, forming a nine-patch.

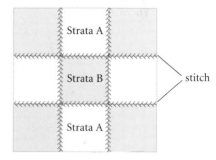

Strata A

Strata B — stitch

Strata A

• Create 12 border blocks.
  - Butt three Strata C segments to the lengthwise edge of one 4" white strip, leaving ½" space between each segment. Stitch, using edge-joining seams.
  - Butt another 4" white strip to the opposite edges of the Strata C segments. Stitch, using edge-joining seams.

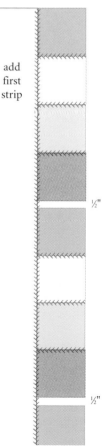

add first strip

add second strip

½"

½"

- Cut the three border blocks apart, following the edges of the Strata C segments.

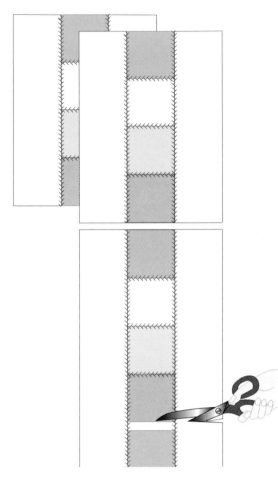

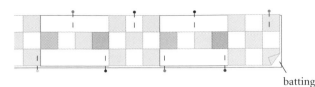

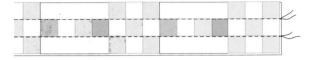
batting

• Stitch in the ditch on each side of the center row, sewing from end to end.

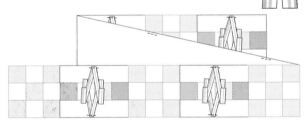

• Repeat, joining the bumper pad back to the second batting section.

8. Add the ties. **10**
  • Fold each 24" long tie in half, meeting the cut edges.
  • Position a tie in the center of the upper and lower edges of each border block on the bumper pad front, aligning the folds of the ties with the raw edges of the bumper pad. Pin baste the tie tails to the center of the bumper pads to prevent them from getting caught in the stitching.
  • Machine baste the folded edges of the ties to the bumper pads, sewing ¼" from the edge.

fold

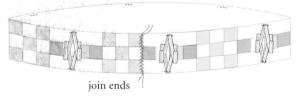
baste ties to both edges

- Repeat with the remaining Strata C segments and 4" white strips, making a total of 12 blocks.

6. Arrange and join the blocks. **30**
  • Join the border blocks and the nine-patch blocks, alternating six nine-patch blocks and six border strata blocks for the front of the bumper pad. Stitch the blocks together using edge-joined seams.

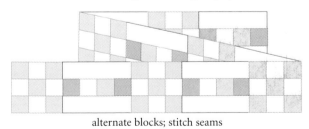
alternate blocks; stitch seams

• Repeat for the back of the bumper pad.

7. Layer and quilt the bumper pad. **30**
  • Cut two batting sections the size of the completed bumper pad front and back.
  • Place one batting section on a flat surface. Position the bumper pad front on the top of the batting, right side up. Pin the layers together.

9. Join the ends of the bumper pad sections. **20**
  • Meet the short edges of the bumper pad front, forming a large circle. Join the edges with an edge-joining seam.

join ends

• Repeat with the bumper pad back.
• Position the bumper pad front over the bumper pad back, meeting the batting sides and aligning the seams at the top and bottom edges. Pin the layers together; then zigzag or straight stitch the edges together.

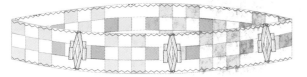

join front and back

10. Bind the bumper pad.   *30*
- Prepare the binding.
  - Join the short ends of three 2" binding strips, right sides together, using a diagonal seam to reduce bulk. Trim the seam; finger or steam press the seam open.

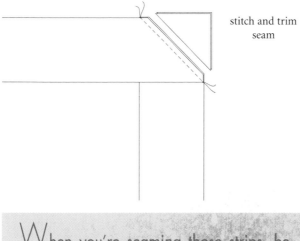

stitch and trim seam

When you're seaming those strips, be sure to join them right sides together. Remember, fleece curls or rolls to the wrong side. If one or more of the strips are joined wrong sides together, the binding will be difficult to apply, since it will curl in the wrong direction.

Nancy

  - Cut one end of the strip at a 45° angle.
- Attach the binding to the quilt.
  - Meet the binding to the right side of the bumper pad, meeting the raw edges and beginning with the angle-cut end. Stitch the binding to the bumper pad with a scant ½" seam, beginning 4" from the end of the binding and stopping 4" from the starting point.

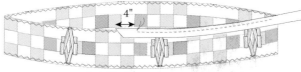

stitch binding to bumper pad

  - Join the binding ends by overlapping the free end of the binding over the beginning of the binding and stitching the ends together with a ¼"

diagonal seam. Trim the excess binding and finger press the seam open. Stitch the remainder of the binding seam.

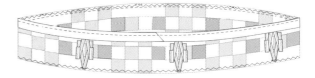

  - Fold the binding over the raw edge. Then fold the binding to the back of the bumper pad, covering the stitching line.
  - Pin the binding in place using Binding and Hem Clips.
  - Secure the remaining edge of the binding by stitching in the ditch from the right side of the bumper pad, sewing in the well of the seam through all the layers to catch the edge on the back side. Or hand stitch the binding edge in place.

fold binding to back; stitch in the ditch

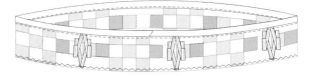

- Repeat, binding the remaining bumper pad edge.

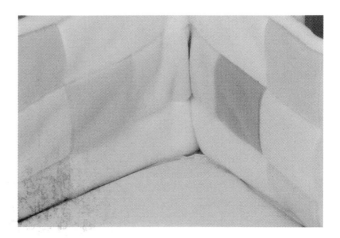

bind lower edge

Babies and soft, cuddly high-loft fleece such as Polarfleece or Polartec just naturally go together. Plus, what toddler doesn't love the feel of a satin binding? This Satin-Edge Baby Blanket is truly speedy to make, yet is a great gift for any new mom and her baby.

FINISHED SIZE

Approximately 36" square

MATERIALS NEEDED

- 1 yd. high-loft fleece
- 5 yd. satin blanket binding

Note: Add a special touch to your blanket with machine embroidery. Select a nursery motif, embroider the baby's name, or choose whatever design you prefer. Instead of hooping the fleece, hoop a sticky-backed stabilizer such as Filmoplast Stic, remove a portion of the paper backing, and position the fleece on the sticky surface. Then embroider the design and remove the fleece from the stabilizer.

Satin-Edge Baby Blanket

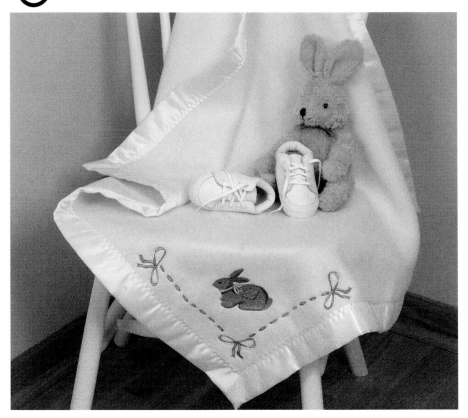

Making the Blanket

1. Square the fleece yardage to 36" x 36". Add 4" to the blanket side measurement. Cut the satin binding into four strips that length (36" + 4" = 40" in this example). **5**

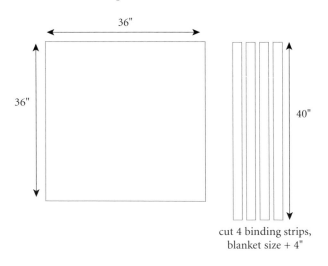

36"

36"

40"

cut 4 binding strips, blanket size + 4"

Although this blanket is 36" square, you can use the same technique to make blankets of other sizes. Since most high-loft fleeces are 60" wide, you have lots of possibilities. You could use a 45" square, a 60" square, or any size you prefer. Just remember to adjust the amount of binding to correspond to the quilt size. Each of the four strips should be 4" longer than the side of the quilt.

Nancy

2. Position the binding strips on the blanket edges. **10**
   - Center the binding strips over the left and right edges, sandwiching the blanket between the binding. Pin.

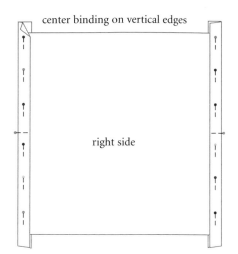

center binding on vertical edges

right side

- On the top and bottom edges, place the binding on top of the blanket, aligning the fold of the binding with the cut edge of the blanket. Pin.

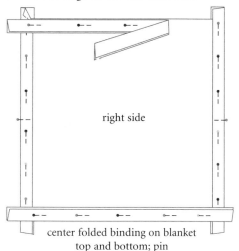

right side

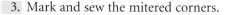

center folded binding on blanket
top and bottom; pin

3. Mark and sew the mitered corners.

15

- Using a washable marking pen, mark each binding at the points where the inner corners meet. Also mark where the outer folded edges meet.

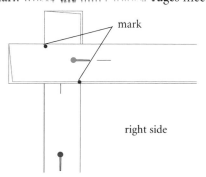

mark

right side

- Transfer the same marking points to the underside of each binding.
- Unpin the bindings only at the corners of the blanket.
- Pin the short ends of the bindings, right sides together, aligning the finished edges and the marks at the folds. Mark the stitching line from the outer marks to the point and back to the outer mark, forming an inverted "V" shape.

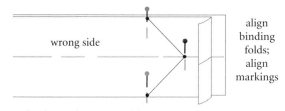

wrong side

align binding folds; align markings

- Stitch along the marked line; trim the excess seam allowances. Press the seam open with a dry iron. Adjust the temperature carefully to avoid damaging the binding.

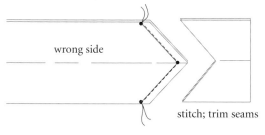

wrong side

stitch; trim seams

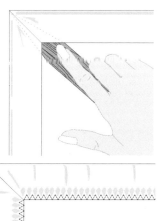

- A small iron such as the Mini Iron® allows you to open the short seams and easily reach into points and corners. The ⅞" x 1⅜" thumb size soleplate reaches areas where larger irons can't fit.
- Turn the blanket corner right side out, using a Bamboo Pointer and Creaser to obtain precise corners. The Bamboo Pointer and Creaser has a pointed end that makes it easy to achieve crisp corners. The opposite curved end helps shape smooth curves and temporarily "presses" seams. Top press using a press cloth.
- Repeat, mitering the remaining three corners.

4. Pin the binding around the blanket. Machine stitch the binding in place using a zigzag or multizigzag stitch.

10

right side

stitch binding in place

Cozy Crib Sheets

Perhaps you've purchased a baby bassinet, cradle, or changing table, and found it difficult to find sheets to fit the mattress. Or maybe you've been fortunate enough to have an heirloom passed down from generation to generation. Instead of searching from store to store to find sheets that fit, sew the sheets. Making custom-made sheets takes very little time, and it's really "sew" easy.

MATERIALS NEEDED

- Fabric (see below to determine amount needed)
- 1 yd. elastic, ¼" to ½" wide

Determining Fabric Requirements

1. Select the fabric for the crib sheet. **5**

Although cotton prints make great sheets, you may want to consider other fabrics as well. For example, use cotton flannel or a cotton knit. These easy-care fabrics are soft and supple, perfect next to baby's delicate skin. If you're working with a knit, it's important to cut the sheet with the length following the more stable lengthwise grain. Cutting the sheet in the opposite direction could save yardage, but the sheet will not fit as well. *Nancy*

2. Prewash the fabric to remove residual shrinkage and any excess sizing or finishes that may have been applied to the fabric at the textile mill. **10**

3. Measure the mattress length, width, and thickness (depth). Determine the fabric required. **10**

- To determine the fabric width needed: Add the mattress width plus twice the mattress depth plus a 3" hem. For example, if the mattress measures 36" x 17" x 3", the width would be 26" (17" width + 6" [2 x 3" depth] + 3" hem).
- To determine the fabric length needed: Add the mattress length plus twice the mattress depth plus a 3" hem. For example, with the dimensions listed above, the cut length would be 45" (36" length + 6" [2 x 3" depth] + 3" hem).
- Therefore, for the mattress described, a 26" x 45" rectangle of fabric would be required.

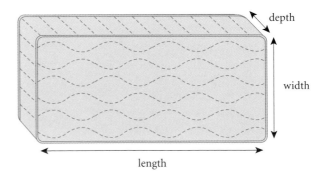

depth

width

length

Making the Sheet

1. Cut a fabric rectangle the size determined on **10** page 88. Shape the sheet corners.
   - Determine the size of corner cutouts by adding 1½" to the mattress depth. For example, if the mattress is 3" deep, the cutout would be 4½" (3" + 1½" = 4½").
   - Fold the fabric in half lengthwise, then crosswise, so all four corners are perfectly stacked.

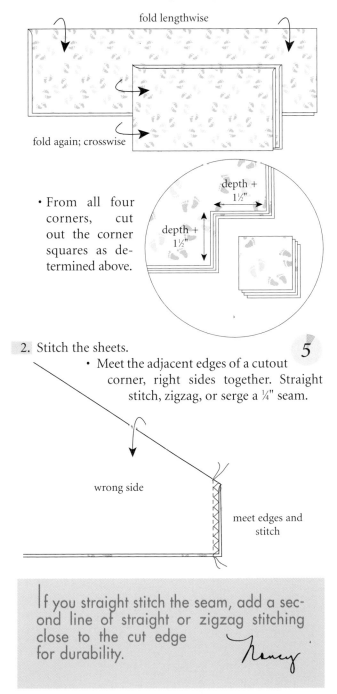

fold lengthwise

fold again; crosswise

depth + 1½"

depth + 1½"

   - From all four corners, cut out the corner squares as determined above.

2. Stitch the sheets. **5**
   - Meet the adjacent edges of a cutout corner, right sides together. Straight stitch, zigzag, or serge a ¼" seam.

wrong side

meet edges and stitch

> If you straight stitch the seam, add a second line of straight or zigzag stitching close to the cut edge for durability. *Nancy*

   - Repeat on the remaining three corners.

3. Add elastic to the corners to make the sheet **15** hug the mattress.
   - Cut four 7" lengths of ¼" to ½" wide elastic. ***Note:*** *For twin or larger sized mattresses, use 9" lengths of elastic.*
   - Fold the elastic in half and mark the center with a washable marking pen.
   - Meet the marked center point to the sheet corner seam on the wrong side of the fabric; pin.
   - Stretch the elastic as far as possible from the center to each end; pin.

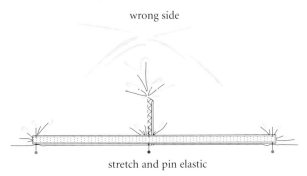

wrong side

stretch and pin elastic

   - Zigzag along the center of the elastic, stretching the elastic to meet the fabric.

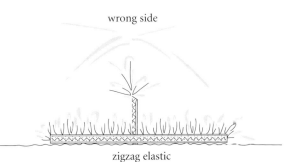

wrong side

zigzag elastic

   - Repeat on the three remaining corners.

4. Hem the sheet. **10**
   - Turn under ½" on the outer edge of the sheet; press.
   - Turn the hem under again, making a double ½" hem. Edgestitch.

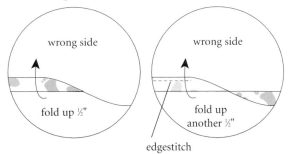

wrong side

fold up ½"

wrong side

fold up another ½"

edgestitch

Techniques

Layering and Quilting

Layering

1. Layer the project, creating a quilt sandwich.
   - Place the backing, wrong side up, on a firm surface.
   - Securely tape the backing to the surface, using Sewer's Fix-it Tape or masking tape.

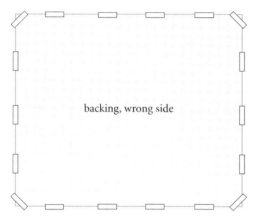

backing, wrong side

   - Center the batting over the backing.
   - Center the project, right side up, over the batting.

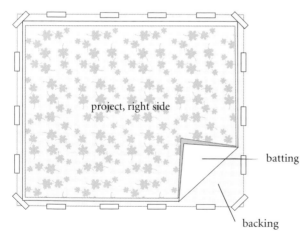

project, right side

batting

backing

2. Pin the layers together.
   - Use size 1 Curved Basting Pins to simplify pinning. These curved nickel-plated brass pins are just the right angle for easy, comfortable insertion, and they won't rust. Pin every 3" to 4".
   - Position the pins no closer than ½" from the seams to allow room for the presser foot when machine quilting.

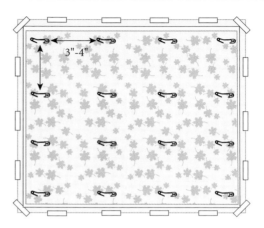

3"-4"

   - Remove the tape.

Quilting

1. Set up the machine for quilting.
   - Attach a quilting bar to the presser foot. This bar makes it easy to space the rows of stitching accurately and uniformly. Adjust the quilting bar so it is 1½" to 2" (or the desired distance) from the needle.

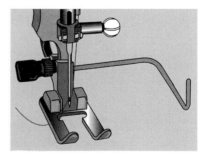

   - Adjust the machine for a straight stitch.
   - Use a balanced tension.
   - Engage the dual feed, or use a Walking Foot so the top and bottom layers feed evenly through the machine. This prevents one layer from shifting and ending up longer than the other.

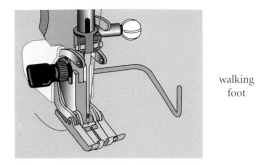

walking
foot

2. Using an erasable fabric marking pen, mark one vertical line and one horizontal line on the quilt sandwich, placing each at the center of the fabric section.

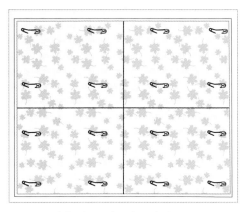

mark horizontal and vertical centers

3. Stitch vertical quilting lines.
   • Straight stitch along the marked vertical line.

stitch vertical row

   • Align and guide the quilting bar along the first row of stitching. Stitch the second row, sewing in the opposite direction of the first row to minimize fabric shifting.

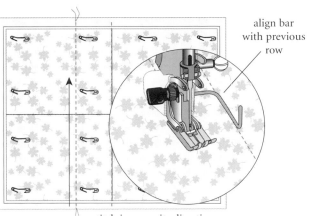

align bar
with previous
row

stitch in opposite direction

   • Repeat, alternating stitching direction with each vertical row. *Note: You may need to reposition the quilting bar so it is to the left of the foot on some rows.*

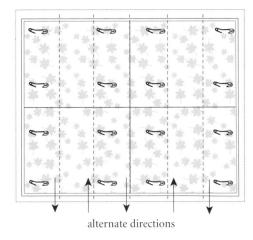

alternate directions

4. Stitch the horizontal rows, using the same technique, again alternating stitching direction with each row.

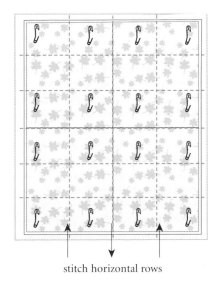

stitch horizontal rows

5. Remove the pins after all stitching is completed.

Making and Applying Bias Tape

When you're applying bias tape, consider all the various possibilities that might be involved in the project. Is the tape applied to a straight or a rounded edge? Does the project include inside or outside corners? Will the ends of the tape be hidden in subsequent seams, or must the ends of the tape be joined to make a continuous edge?

Analyze your project, and before beginning, read the sections of these instructions that apply to that project. Then refer back to those instructions as you make your project. For example, if you need to join tape ends, you'll want to add paper-backed fusible web to the end of the tape before applying the tape.

Thoroughly reviewing the process before you start will save time and effort later on.

Making Bias Tape

1. Cut bias strips of the width indicated for the project.

2. Join the short ends of the strips, right sides together, with diagonal seams to reduce bulk. Create a length of tape as indicated for each project. Trim the seam allowances.

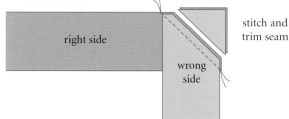

right side

wrong side

stitch and trim seam

3. Press the seams open.

wrong side

4. Advance the tape through a Bias Tape Maker, wrong side up, creating wide single fold bias tape. Use a 1" Tape Maker with 2" strips, and a ¾" Tape Maker with 1½" strips.

Applying Bias Tape: Two-Step Method

1. Unfold one of the pressed edges of the bias tape. Pin the tape to the outer edge of the project, meeting the cut edges, placing the right side of the tape on the wrong side of the project. Stitch in the pressed fold of the binding.

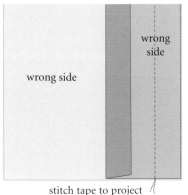

wrong side

wrong side

stitch tape to project

2. Fold the binding to the right side of the project, aligning the fold of the binding to cover the first stitching line.

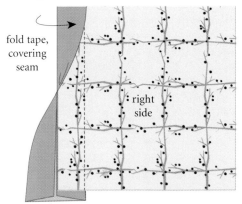

fold tape, covering seam

right side

3. Edgestitch the binding in place.

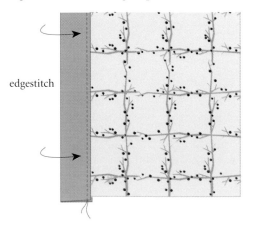

edgestitch

Applying Bias Tape: One-Step Method

1. This technique is appropriate for binding straight or gently curved edges, but it doesn't work with square or mitered corners.

2. Replace the conventional presser foot with a Bias Binder Foot. This foot has an adjustable guide that folds the bias tape around the fabric edge as you stitch. The guide can be adjusted from 5mm to 20mm to simultaneously sew straight, even rows of stitching on both folded edges of bias tape wrapped around an edge. There's no need to sew twice.

3. Bind the edge.
   - Set the machine for a straight stitch with a center needle position.
   - Fold the single fold bias tape, meeting the outer edges, to create a double fold tape. Press the fold.

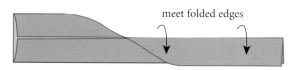

meet folded edges

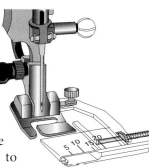

- Insert the prefolded bias tape through the opening in the front of the foot so the folded edges fit in the curved upper and lower guides at the left of the foot.

adjust screw 1

insert bias tape

- Turn screw 1 until the ends of the bias binding butt against the outer edges of the curved guides.
- Gently lift the upper curved guide and insert the fabric to be bound, right side up, between the two guides, making sure the fabric is inserted the full width of the binding.

- Adjust the front guide with screw 1 if necessary to accommodate the fabric layers.

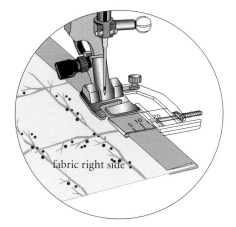

fabric right side

- Lower the Bias Binder Foot and turn the flywheel by hand until the needle is just above the fabric. Adjust the back guide with screw 2 to position the needle at the desired distance from the binding edge.

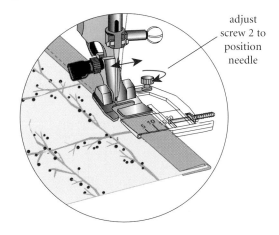

adjust screw 2 to position needle

- Work with a 6" to 8" section of fabric and binding at a time. Encase the fabric edge with the prefolded bias tape and sew, feeding the section through the Bias Binder Foot. Repeat until the entire edge is bound.
- To apply binding to gentle curves, preshape the binding with steam before stitching.

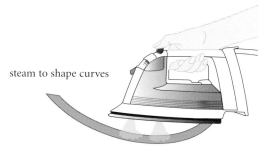

steam to shape curves

Mitering Outside Corners

1. Use the Two-Step Method. Mark ½" (or the distance indicated in the project) from each corner.

wrong side

mark each corner

2. Unfold one edge of the bias tape; meet the right side of the tape to the wrong side of the project, aligning the cut edges. Stitch to the first mark. Lock the stitches.

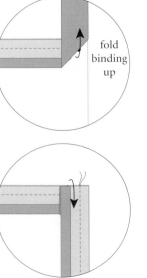

stop stitching at mark

wrong side

- Fold the tape up so the cut edge aligns with the cut edge of the project.
- Fold the binding down, meeting the tape fold to the top of the corner and the tape cut edge to the side edge. Stitch the side, beginning at the folded edge.
- Repeat at the remaining corner(s). If appropriate, join the tape ends as indicated on page 95.

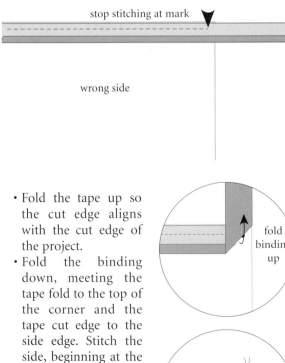

fold binding up

fold binding down; stitch

- Fold the tape to the right side, aligning the pressed edge so it covers the stitching line and tucking the corners to form miters. Edgestitch the tape in place.

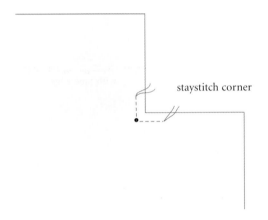

edgestitch

Binding Inside Corners

1. Use the Two-Step Method.

2. Mark ½" from each corner. Staystitch the inner corner, sewing a scant ½" from the cut edges.

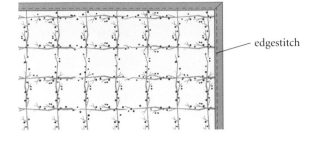

staystitch corner

3. Clip into the interior corners without cutting through the staystitching.

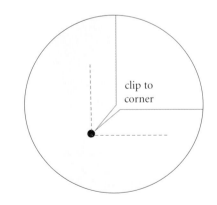

clip to corner

4. Join the binding to the project.
- Unfold one edge of the bias tape. Meet the right side of the tape to the wrong side of the project, aligning the cut edges. Stitch to the marked point, stopping with the needle down in the fabric.

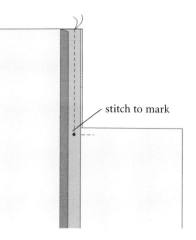

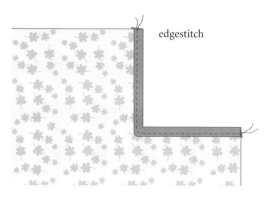

edgestitch

- Gently pivot the fabric under the bias tape so the second side of the fabric corner aligns with the edge of the tape.
- Continue stitching to the next corner mark.

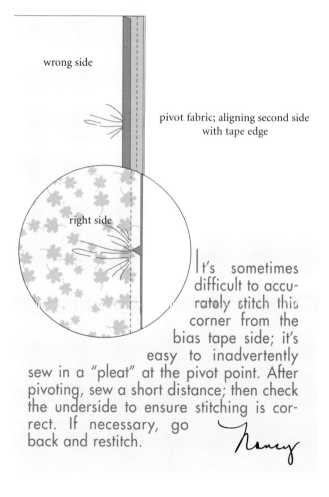

wrong side

pivot fabric; aligning second side with tape edge

right side

It's sometimes difficult to accurately stitch this corner from the bias tape side; it's easy to inadvertently sew in a "pleat" at the pivot point. After pivoting, sew a short distance; then check the underside to ensure stitching is correct. If necessary, go back and restitch.

Nancy

- Repeat the steps at the remaining corners, using the technique for an outside or inside corner as appropriate.
- Fold the binding to the right side of the project so it covers the first stitching. Edgestitch to secure the tape.

Joining Tape Ends

When bias tape is applied around the edge of a rectangular or circular item, you need to join the ends of the bias. Here's an easy way to get a smooth, bulk-free joining.

1. Open the bias tape. Cut the starting end of the tape at a 45° angle, using a rotary cutter, mat, and quilting ruler. Press under ¼" at the trimmed end of the tape.

cut 45° angle, fold in ¼"

wrong side

2. Cut a ¼" strip of paper-backed fusible web. Press the strip to the folded-under edge of the binding. Refold the binding.

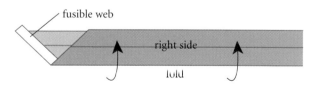

fusible web

right side

fold

3. Pin the binding to the project, starting in the center of one side. Begin stitching 3" to 4" from the cut end of the tape.

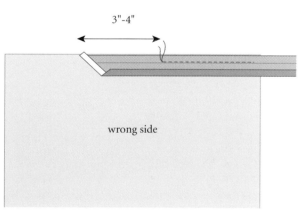

3"-4"

wrong side

4. Attach the bias as detailed for the Two-Step Method. Stop stitching 3" before the start of the tape. A 6" to 7" section will remain unstitched.

5. Remove the paper backing from the fusible web at the beginning end of the binding. Nest the second end of the bias inside the beginning of the strip; press in place.

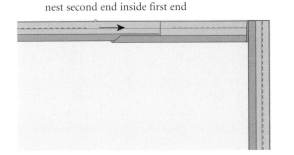

nest second end inside first end

6. Trim off the excess bias tape from the end of the tape.

7. Stitch the two tape ends together, following the crease mark.

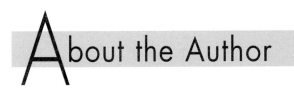

stitch remaining section

8. Align the unsewn portion of the bias tape to the mat. Finish sewing the unstitched section.

9. Fold the tape to the right side, aligning the pressed tape edge so it covers the stitching line. Edgestitch the tape in place.

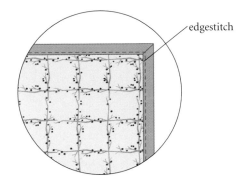

edgestitch

About the Author

Nancy Zieman is a national sewing authority, business-woman, author, pattern designer, and home economist, as well as the executive producer and host of the popular PBS television show, *Sewing With Nancy*. This is her 17th book. Her recent book, *Sewing With Nancy's Favorite Hints*, is a compilation of viewer hints from 20 years of her television program. The book is available from Krause Publications or Nancy's Notions.